# CHAPMAN'S

## Nautical Guides

# *Communications Afloat*

D0972555

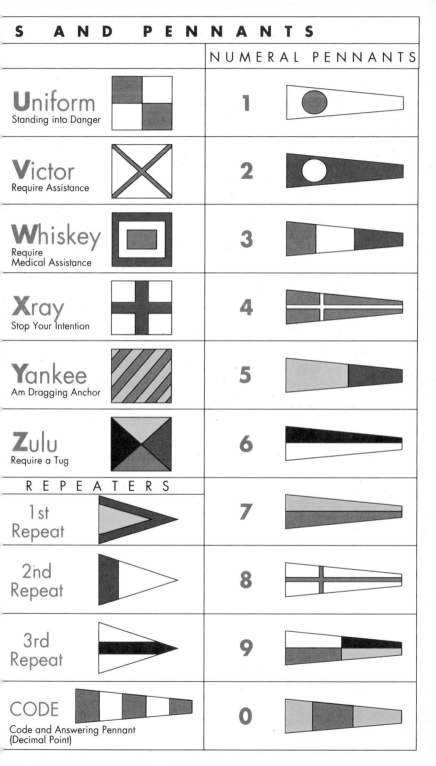

# Communications Afloat

*by Elbert S. Maloney*
*illustrations by Ralph Futrell*

**HEARST MARINE BOOKS**
**New York**

Recognizing the importance of preserving what has been written, it is the
policy of William Morrow and Company, Inc., and its imprints and affiliates
to have the books it publishes printed on acid-free paper, and we exert our
best efforts to that end.

Library of Congress Catalog Card Number: 90-81986

ISBN: 0-688-09823-1

Printed in Italy
First U.S. Edition
1 2 3 4 5 6 7 8 9 10

Edited by Lucy A. O'Brien
Produced by Smallwood and Stewart Inc.
9 West 19th Street
New York, N.Y. 10011

# CONTENTS

# INTRODUCTION

Think of your boat as a small floating island in the midst of a big sea. Around you are other floating boat-islands, some near and some far, each populated with a handful of people who, like all islanders, need to call for help in times of distress or medical emergency, contact each other and the mainland for social and personal reasons, and generally not feel isolated, knowing that someone is watching out for their welfare.

The analogy between inhabiting an island and being afloat is something that everyone who has ever been at sea in a sailing vessel or a powerboat understands. In the days before electronics, vessels communicated with each other by flag and semaphore signals and megaphones, necessarily at short distances. Vessels in distress flew their national ensigns upside down or burned oily rags to create smudge (they still do). The first, primitive transmitter and receiver was put aboard a merchant liner around the turn of the century. With Morse code as the medium, the operator was able, finally, to communicate with other ships. Today, the ocean is spanned by advanced marine electronics descended from the original transmitter and receiver.

Communication by radio today is an integral part of being afloat. No prudent skipper would embark on a coastal cruise or even take a turn on home waters without VHF radio on board. Nor would he or she venture far offshore without single-sideband (SSB) and/or ham radio. With satellite communications, you can bridge great spans of sky and ocean at a double bound. If you are in trouble, radio position-locating equipment can save your life. This book will help you understand this gear and how to use it.

**The Two Uses of Communications Afloat**

There are two major reasons for communications afloat : safety and convenience. Safety, of course, is paramount, but you will be surprised at the extent to which the reliability and ease of communicating from your boat via VHF or SSB will add also to your convenience and pleasure.

Safety communications range from the prosaic, such as weather forecasts or the latest Broadcast Notice to Mariners, to extreme emergency (Mayday) situations, such as sinking, fire, or severe medical problems. Safety messages come first: The Rules and Regulations of the Federal Communications Commission (FCC) give absolute priority to distress communcations.

The FCC is pretty clear, as well, about communications of convenience. They must be necessary—that is, they must be communications that cannot be delayed until they can be carried out by other means, such as land telephone or mail or face-to-face. The FCC rules expressly prohibit "superfluous radio communications," although the term is not defined. Within these limitations, for instance, you can call a marina requesting information on fuel or dock space, but if you ask what the marina restaurant has on the menu for dinner, you may be in trouble with the FCC. Social conversation is not allowed between boats either. There are two exceptions to these limitations, however: Conversations on "public correspondence" channels (ship-to-shore) are unrestricted except by FCC rules against obscenity, and communications via citizens band (CB) radio are also mainly unrestricted .

**Radio Waves**

For most of us radio waves are a mysterious phenomenon. Unlike ocean waves, radio waves are invisible; yet they undoubtedly exist, as evidenced by the transmission and reception of radio and television signals. Simply stated, radio waves are electromagnetically propagated by the reversal of electrical current at an antenna, from which they move outward in all directions. When you change the rate of the reversals, waves of different lengths are generated. If you could see them, radio waves would look like waves of the sea —short and more frequent, like chop waves, or long and less frequent, like ocean waves that have traveled over great distances. Because all radio waves travel at the same speed, the more waves per second (frequency), the shorter they are, the fewer per second, the longer they are in the spectrum of radio waves.

Frequency is measured in units called Hertz (named after one of the great pioneers in electromagnetic theory). Marine radio communications use frequencies measured mainly in kiloHertz (1000 Hertz), and megaHertz (1000 kiloHertz), the accepted abbreviations for which are kHz and MHz. Segments of the radio spectrum—frequency bands—have been assigned tasks for which they are the most useful. Although there are other, higher and lower frequency bands, those used in marine radio systems are the following:

| | |
|---|---|
| Very Low Frequency (VLF) | 3-30kHz |
| Low Frequency (LF) | 30-300 kHz |
| Medium Frequency (MF) | 300-3000 kHz (3 MHz) |
| High Frequency (HF) | 3-30 MHz |
| Very High Frequency (VHF) | 30-300 MHz |
| Ultra High Frequency (UHF) | 300-3000 MHz (3 GHz) |

How radio waves travel outward from a transmitting antenna is determined by their frequency and by the physical and electrical characteristics of that antenna. In broad terms, waves of lower frequency tend to follow around the curvature of the earth, as ground waves. These are absorbed by the earth and steadily decrease in strength as the distance from the point of origin increases. On the other hand, as the frequency of the ground waves increases, the distance traveled decreases. Higher frequency signals have some limited ground wave coverage, but they basically tend to go out at angles above the horizon, with a large portion of their radio-frequency energy being reflected back by layers of ionization that are tens to hundreds of miles above the earth's surface. Higher frequency signals are sky waves, and they make long-distance radio communications practicable. In the space between the transmission

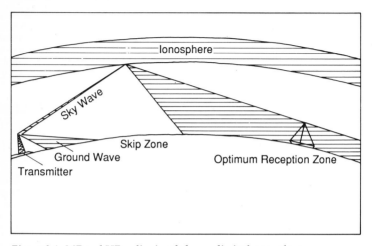

*Figure 0.1 MF and HF radio signals have a limited ground wave range covering a few hundred miles. They are also reflected by the ionoshpere and return to earth farther out as sky waves. Between the reception zones of ground and sky waves is the "skip zone," an area of no signals.*

point and the sky-wave reception point, you will not hear the signals—this is the skip zone; the wave will have bounced off the ionosphere at an angle and returned to earth at that angle, leaving a dead reception space between. In general, higher frequencies are used for longer distances and may have a greater skip zone. Skip distances and sky-wave transmission and reception vary with the time of day, the season, and even the state of the sunspot cycle.

**Primary Power Sources**

The generation of radio signals requires a source of primary power, as does the operation of equipment to receive the signals. The power required is electrical—on boats this is usually 12 volts DC; larger vessels and shore installations may use higher DC voltages or AC power. Lead-acid storage batteries are a boat's source of power; actual operation is at about 13.2 volts, although the term "12-volt" is common usage. The electrical power consumed by a

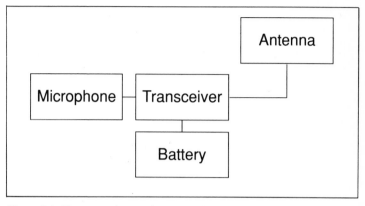

*Figure 0.2  The transmitter and receiver of a marine radio are usually combined into a "transceiver." To complete the installation, there must be a source of electrical power (battery), a microphone, and an antenna; MF and HF sets also require a ground system.*

marine radio is greater when transmitting than receiving and can be depleted if not kept charged.

Hand-held radios (and other portable electronic communications equipment) are normally powered by internal storage batteries of the rechargeable nickel-cadmium (Ni-Cad) type. Depending upon the accessories available for the set, these batteries can be recharged from either a 12-volt DC source or a 120-volt AC line.

Reliable communications depend upon there being an adequately charged source of primary power, whether it is lead-acid storage batteries or internal Ni-Cads.

**Organization of This Book**

This book covers communications by radio and by other means to and from a vessel, as well as within it. In recognition of its primary role, VHF-FM radio is considered first, followed by other forms of marine radio communications, single-sideband (SSB) on the MF and HF bands, citizens band (CB), and amateur (ham) radio. Also included are communications via cellular telephones, satellite communications, and emergency position-indicating radiobeacons

**11**

(EPIRBs). Rounding out this look at communications afloat are brief discussions of visual and nonelectronic aural signaling, and internal communications .

The primary focus of this book is on small craft, both commercial and recreational. However, Rules and Regulations of the FCC covering what is termed the "Maritime Mobile Service" largely apply to all vessels regardless of size; to a surprising extent, the equipment is the same.

# CHAPTER ONE

# VHF RADIO

T he most important piece of communications gear on your boat is your VHF radio. With it you can call for help, converse with other yachts, and talk to bridge tenders, commercial ships, and towboats with a half-mile of barges in tow. You can listen to weather forecasts and call home. With VHF radio you are secure aboard your vessel, certain that Coast Guard stations and vessels within 20 miles of you (or more, depending upon antenna height) can always be reached. Since VHF radio waves are line-of-sight and cling to the earth's surface, they a re not much affected by weather or atmospheric conditions. And because they are frequency-modulated (FM) by changes in the signal generation, voice propagation is relatively interference free.

It is important to remember, however, that the small VHF transceiver on your boat is actually part of a system with channels for broadcasting and receiving, priorities and methods for using those channels, and classes of authorized users. Working your VHF set is easy, but to operate it efficiently and lawfully you must understand all parts of the system.

## A Bit of History

VHF-FM radio came into wide use in the early 1970's, mainly because of an untenable situation in the marine airwaves. Only four shortwave AM channels were available for use by boats, with one or two more for ship-to-shore traffic. Of these channels, only two were available for recreational boat-to-boat communications. Since these were between 2 and 3 MHz, the range for each boat's radio was roughly 50 to 100 miles. It is not hard to imagine how over-crowded—to the point of chaos—the airwaves became on weekends with good boating weather, when hundreds of boats were within radio range of each other. The creation of the VHF service was truly a blessing for boaters.

**About VHF Radio**

The radio frequencies used in the VHF marine band lie between 156 and 158 MHz, with some shore stations available between 161 and 163 MHz. Within this band, specific frequencies are designated "channels," as is done with television and citizens band radio, so that each channel has its assigned frequency, or pair of frequencies. Originally the spacing between adjacent channels was 50 kHz for Channels 1 through 28. Later, as equipment design improved, additional channels were interleaved (Channels 61 through 88) and ten were designated weather channels, so the spacing is now 25 kHz. Not all channels are used, and allocations in the United States may be different from international allocations. However, U.S. channel numbers are all that you probably will need to know, and all that will be discussed from here on. (You will have to know frequencies, rather than channel numbers, to tune shortwave receivers and scanners; see Appendix A.)

The Marine VHF band provides communications over distances that are essentially "line-of-sight." Actual transmission range will depend much more on antenna type and height than on the power of the transmitter. The marine frequencies lie in a gap between television Channels 6 and 7 and are generally subject to the same range limitations. Communications can be carried on over distances somewhat greater than true optical line-of-sight, but the added range is usually not more than 25 percent, if that much. This is for "normal" conditions. There will be times of freak atmospheric conditions when VHF signals may be heard from as far away as 200 or 300 miles, but reliable communications will rarely be possible in such circumstances, nor is it possible to predict such conditions in advance.

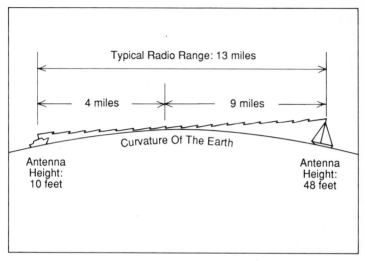

*Figure 1.1 Antenna height is significant in the VHF range signals. The ranges shown above are approximate and are about 10% greater than the distance to the visible horizon, to allow for the slight bending that occurs with radio waves.*

**Some Definitions You Need to Know**

FCC rules and regulations governing the marine VHF system are fundamentally based on the type of vessel. The FCC uses the following definitions of categories of vessels, stations, and types of communications to regulate VHF radio.

*Voluntary ship*: (All vessels are defined as "ships.") One which carries a radio but is not required to have one. If there is only one communications radio on board it must be VHF. All recreational boats fit into this category, as do vessels for hire carrying less than six passengers.

*Compulsory ship*: A vessel required by law or treaty to have a radio installation. Small vessels for hire carrying more than six passengers are included in this category.

*Commercial transport vessel*: A ship used primarily in commerce transporting persons or goods to and from ports. The category, however, also includes commercial fishing craft and sightseeing boats carrying more than six passengers.

*Ship station*: A radio installation aboard a vessel of any size that is not permanently moored.

*Coast station*: A land-based station in the maritime radio service.

*Public coast (correspondence) station*: A land radiotelephone station (Marine Operator) that is open to calls from all vessels requiring access to a land telephone system.

*Private coast station*: A station located in a yacht club, marina, restaurant, towing service, and so forth, that serves the needs of private vessels.

*Safety communications*: Distress, urgent, and safety traffic or any form of radio communication that, if delayed, might adversely affect the safety of life or property.

*Commercial communications*: Transmissions between commercial transport vessels or between such vessels and coast stations that relate directly to the purpose for which the vessel is used. These include piloting, movement of vessels, obtaining vessel supplies, and the scheduling of repairs.

*Noncommercial communications*: Conversations that relate to the "needs" of the ship.

### Who May Use VHF?

All persons and vessels licensed by the FCC plus designated shore stations and certain government stations, such as units of the Coast Guard that are not required to have licenses, may use VHF. Remember, you may not legally transmit on VHF radio without a station license.

The skipper of a voluntarily equipped vessel is not required to have a copy of the FCC rules, but it is not a bad idea! Copy or no copy, he or she is required to know the Rules and Regulations, and to comply with them. You probably will have to write to the Government Printing Office, Washington, DC 20402, or to a GPO Regional Bookstore, to get a copy; ask for *Code of Federal Regulations, Title 47, Part 80*.

## "Calling" and "Working" Channels

A basic characteristic of VHF Marine Radiotelephone System is the use of separate "calling" and "working" channels. In any given vicinity where all boats can hear each other—a roughly circular area of perhaps 15 to 20 miles in radius—each channel is like the old-fashioned party line; everyone can hear what the others say, and only one person at a time can speak. With many channels to choose from, this might not be so much of a problem, but how would you know which channel to use to call a vessel with which you wanted to establish contact? The solution is to have one channel designated for calling only and to use others to actually carry on the conversation. Each skipper listens on the "calling channel" (Channel 16) when not actively communicating with another station (or receiving weather or Coast Guard broadcasts), so that is where you will find him or her when you want to talk! By quickly changing to a "working channel" for the conversation, you free up the calling channel for calls by others. With boats shifting to various working channels, there should be little or no crowding on any one of them.

A second aspect of this calling/working procedure is that the calling channel (16), is also used for distress signals. With all vessels that are not actively engaged in communications listening on this channel, there is a much increased likelihood of a distress call being heard and answered.

FCC regulations require that all radios be tuned to Channel 16 when they are not being actively used for communications. Occasionally boats in a cruising group will keep their radios tuned to a working channel rather than Channel 16. This is in violation of the FCC rules and defeats the system, which takes the safety of all boaters into account.

# CHAPTER TWO

# VHF CHANNEL ASSIGNMENTS

T
he VHF system is well designed to spread the load of traffic among the 55 different channels (out of 78) accessible to the American mariner so that interference is minimized and you have a channel available when you need one. But to make the system work, channels must be used according to their intended purpose by those for whom the specific channel is allocated. (Turn to Appendix A for a complete list of channels and authorized uses and users.)

Let us consider these channels in their order of importance to the recreational boater. The first two channels, 16 and 06, are required by the FCC to be installed in every VHF transceiver (in addition to one working channel selected by the licensee).

### The International Distress and Calling Channel: 16

VHF Channel 16 is located approximately in the middle of the VHF marine band, at 156.800 MHz, and is assigned by international treaty to be used only for distress, urgent, and safety communications, and for initial calls to establish contact with another boat or the Coast Guard. These are the only authorized uses for this channel. Any other use, no matter how brief, is prohibited. In addition, all recreational and "compulsorily equipped" vessels are required to monitor Channel 16 when their radios are on and they are not communicating on another channel.

VHF coast stations serving rivers, bays, and lakes—except the Great Lakes—must maintain a watch on Channel 16 unless specifically exempted by the FCC. This provides coverage where there are few, if any, Coast Guard stations.

*Figure 2.1  The desired channel on a VHF set can be selected by rotating a knob, by pressing buttons on a key pad, or on some hand-held sets, by rotating a pair of thumbwheels.*

There are a few very specific exceptions to this requirement for monitoring Channel 16, and most of these are not generally applicable to recreational small craft. A voluntarily equipped vessel that has digital selective calling (DSC) equipment may maintain a continuous watch on Channel 70 instead of Channel 16, but only while within the VHF service area of a Coast Guard station that is DSC equipped. A vessel that is subject to the Bridge-to-Bridge Radiotelephone Act and is participating in a Vessel Traffic Service (VTS) system need not guard Channel 16 if it is maintaining a watch on both the Bridge-to-Bridge and VTS frequencies.

### The Intership Safety Channel: 06

Channel 06, also required on every VHF set, is the intership safety channel to be used for priority and urgent traffic relating to the safety of vessels. (Note that "intership" is the term that the FCC uses to refer to communications between vessels of all types, including recreational boats. This term and "ship-to-ship" are used interchangeably.)

The idea is to have one dedicated channel available that all vessels can switch to in safety situations after the initial contact is made on Channel 16, so that 16 can be left free for other safety communications and initial contact calls. According to the FCC rules, Channel 06 is reserved for use by vessels afloat—no shore stations may use it—and it may only be used for safety communications.

(You may have noticed what appears to be a discrepancy in the use of double and single digits (6 or 06) below 10 on your VHF channel selector or in the literature. Both are correct. Most sets on which the channel number is entered with a key pad require two digits. Some VHF radios are designed so that a single-digit entry brings up a weather channel and a two-digit entry calls up a working channel.)

**The Coast Guard Working Channel: 22A**

Channel 22A is the frequency restricted to Coast Guard use for safety communications of all sorts, including responses to distress calls. Once contact with the Coast Guard is made on Channel 16, the station will request that you switch to Channel 22A to determine your problem. In case of overloaded traffic on Channel 22A, you may be asked to return to the Coast Guard station on Channel 12, which is normally a port-operations frequency (one used for communications relative to the handling, movement, and safety of ships in or near a port, at canal locks, and in waterways).

The suffix "A" means that the channel has a split frequency capability. In this case, Channel 22 is used overseas for ship-to-shore communications, with the ship frequency being different from the shore frequency (duplex), while in the United States (22A) the sending and receiving frequencies are the same (simplex). This can lead to confusion when a mariner buys a VHF radio equipped with a switch that programs the set for international or U.S. channels. If the switch is set for international frequencies, the radio will not receive transmissions destined for U.S. Channel 22A.

## Noncommercial Ship-to-Ship Working Channels:
### 09, 68, 69, 71, 72, 78A

These six channels are authorized for communications between recreational vessels. You will find that there is no preference for use other than switching to the one that is least congested. The most congested is usually Channel 68, a holdover from the early days of VHF when sets were "crystal-controlled"—they could only transmit and receive on channels for which a pair of quartz crystals tuned to that frequency were installed. (Today's sets are "synth-esized"—drawing off one master crystal.) As most sets were limited to a maximum of twelve channels (to keep the cost down, many had six or eight), only one or two ship-to-ship working frequencies could be included. To insure that there would be at least one common working channel, 68 became standard on every set. Thus the habit of "switching to 68" was established and continues today. The other working channels are equally available, and greater use of them would do much to relieve congestion on 68.

### Joint Commercial/ Noncommercial Vessel Working Channel: 09

There is a channel, just one, that is authorized for intership use for *both* commercial and noncommercial vessels; this is Channel 09. In the FCC rules, this is simply listed as one of the authorized working channels in the listing for commercial ships and again in the listing of working channels for noncommercial ships (always remember that to the FCC, boats are "ships"). By virtue of the double listing, however, it is the obvious channel for intercommunications between the two different categories of vessels.

### Communications to Private Coast Stations: 09, 68, 69, 71, 78A

Some, but not all, of the intership channels are also authorized for use between vessels and private coast stations, typically marinas and yacht clubs, or the bases of small-craft towing services. For noncom-mercial communications, the channels that can be used are 09, 68, 69, 71, and 78A; Channel 72 is specifically excluded from such use.

## The Bridge-to-Bridge Channels: 13, 67

These working channels are for communication between the navigation bridges and helm stations of vessels—the place where quick action can be taken when a safety problem arises. The FCC authorized the channels, the Coast Guard mandated their use and prescribed the vessel-to-vessel procedures. The thought on the part of the Coast Guard was that collisions would be avoided and far greater safety achieved if the persons controlling the movements of vessels approaching or overtaking one another could communicate by voice rather than whistle signals. As any yacht skipper who has been contacted by the captain of an approaching tow knows, the procedure has proven to work very well.

In certain specifically defined waterways, such as the New Orleans Vessel Traffic Service Protection area run by the Coast Guard, Channel 67 is designated for Bridge-to-Bridge communication instead of Channel 13.

The requirement to maintain a watch on Channel 13 (or, where appropriate, Channel 67) is placed only on certain categories of vessels by regulations of the U.S. Coast Guard. These are: (1) all power-driven vessels of 300 or more gross tons; (2) all vessels of 100 or more tons if carrying one or more passengers for hire; (3) all towing vessels 26 or more feet in length; and (4) all dredges and other "floating plant" in or near a channel or fairway, if their operation is likely to restrict or affect the navigation of other vessels. Vessels required to maintain a Bridge-to-Bridge radio watch must have on board at least one person having a Restricted Radiotelephone Operator Permit or higher-class license (see Chapter 3). A specific person must be designated to maintain the Bridge-to-Bridge watch, but that person may have other duties if such do not interfere with the radio watch. Vessels not required to guard Channel 13 (67) may listen if they so desire—but not in lieu of monitoring Channel 16.

Another use for Channel 13 developed later. In many areas, highway and railroad bridges are equipped with VHF radios and use Channel 13 for dialogue with oncoming vessels. Here again, voice exchanges enable better communications than whistle signals.

The need of an approaching vessel for the bridge to open can be communicated from a greater distance, which is highly desirable in conditions of strong currents. Information on the inability of a bridge to be opened immediately can be passed, with reasons for and probable length of delay.

The FCC rules normally limit the power on Channel 13 (67) to 1 watt; this is often designated as "low power" on sets. If absolutely necessary, the power at stations on vehicle bridges may be increased to 10 watts, or to 25 watts on ship stations (boats are not capable of setting the power to 10 watts—it is either 1 or 25).

### Port-Operations Channels: 01, 05, 12, 14, 20, 20A, 63, 65, 66, 73, 74, 77

The FCC defines "port-operations communications" as those between vessels or between a vessel and a coast station that relate to the operational handling, movement, and safety of ships in or near a port, at canal locks, and in waterways. Specific channels are assigned for such contacts. Channels 12 and 14 are the most commonly employed, while 01, 05, 20 (20A for intership use), 63, 65, 66, 73, 74, and 77 (77 is intership only) are also authorized, but much less frequently used. There are geographical restrictions on some of these port-operations channels. These channels are primarily used by harbor-control authorities and ship pilots.

### Marine Channels for Aircraft Use: 06, 08, 09, 16, 18, 22A, 67, 68, 72, 88

Under certain conditions, aircraft may use marine VHF channels for communications with vessels. Communications must be limited to operations in which the vessel is primarily involved, and where direct air-surface communications are required. Of the authorized channels, 06 and 16 have the same restrictions as for vessels, and Channels 22A, 67, and 88 have geographic limitations. Transmitter power on the aircraft must be limited to 5 watts. Aircraft must not be more than 1,000 feet above the water, except for reconnaissance aircraft involved in icebreaking operations, where 1,500 feet altitude is allowed.

**Public Correspondence Channels: 24, 25, 26, 27, 28, 84, 85, 86, 87, 88**

Public coast stations are operated by the Bell System and by independent companies so that vessels can make calls to shore and these can then be "patched" into the nationwide, even worldwide, telephone network. In the language of the FCC, this is "public correspondence" communications. Separate channels are provided for this service, each consisting of a pair of frequencies. The vessel transmits on one frequency and the shore station on the other; such alternating transmissions are termed "half-duplex." In most cases, if you are speaking from a boat, you cannot be interrupted by the person at the shore station, for your receiver is disabled as long as you have your microphone button pressed to send. Some newer sets allow "full-duplex," in which either person can interrupt the other as if they were speaking on a land telephone. Marine Operators are allocated channels geographically, with Channels 26 and 28 being the most widely assigned (this is another holdover from the days of limited channel availability on early VHF sets). In most areas, a single channel is assigned to a given marine radiotelephone shore station, but in locations of heavy traffic additional channels can be allocated.

**Government Channels: 17, 21A, 22A, 23A, 81A, 82A, 83A**

In addition to the channels allocated to ships and boats by the FCC, there are six government channels under the control of the Coast Guard. Although your radio may have the capability of transmitting on these channels, you must *not* do so unless specifically directed to by a Coast Guard station. Remember, the "A" in each channel designation means that the radio must be programmed to U.S. channels. Check the switch on the front panel.

Channel 17 is designated for "Maritime Control" and is available for use by state and local governments, which may employ it in their search-and-rescue training exercises.

## Weather Channels: WX-1, WX-2, WX-3

Several receive-only channels are allocated to the National Oceanic and Atmospheric Administration (NOAA) for the continuous broadcast of weather information. The channels are assigned geographically to minimize interference.

## The Special Case of Channel 70

We have saved discussion of this channel allocation for last because it is being used for the development of a new high-tech form of marine communications called Digital Selective Calling (DSC), which is aimed at doing away with the "party line" phenomena of such services as the public correspondence (Marine Operator) channels. Until September 1985, Channel 70 was authorized for noncommercial intership use, but then, by international treaty, it was withdrawn by the United States and set aside for DSC. Transceivers with the capability of receiving and transmitting DSC signals are just beginning to come on the market at this time (1990), and the prices are well above those of the best sets that do not contain this feature. The main thing to know about Channel 70 is that trying to use it as an intership talk channel is illegal.

# CHAPTER THREE

# LICENSES FOR VHF MARINE RADIO OPERATION

Licenses for operating a radio transmitter—none is required for just a receiver—follow the same pattern as for automobiles. There are two separate licenses involved—one for the equipment (corresponding to car registration) and one for the operator (similar to a vehicle driver's permit). You must have *both* for legal operation of your transceiver. They are issued by the FCC and may be obtained by mail.

On 21 May 1990, the FCC established a schedule of fees for certain radio permits and licenses, as required by U.S. Congressional action, plus a set of complicated procedures for their payment. Many fees are $35, the minimum set by Congress; this will be revised every two years to keep up with changes in the Consumer Price Index for all Urban Consumers (CPI-U), or further Congressional action. Now, in addition to the application form for the permit or license, you must also submit a fee processing form, FCC Form 155. Use Section I of this form if you are applying for one action only, such as the issuance of an operator permit. Since only one Form 155 is to be sent with each submission, use Section II if your application requires two or more fees, such as applying for an operator permit and a station license at the same time. An important element of this form is the "Fee Type Code." The regulations state: "A wrong Fee Type Code or incorrect remittance may result in your application being returned without processing." A single check or money order, in U.S. funds, payable to the Federal Communications Commission, must be included; do not send cash. Finally, the regulations instruct, "do not staple the check to the application or fee processing form. Failure to abide by these instructions will delay the processing of your submission."

# Operator Permits and Licenses

FCC Radiotelephone Operator authorizations are issued in grades—the lower grades are termed "permits" and the highest grade is a "license." Uncorrected physical handicaps are not a bar to the issuance of a license, but appropriate restrictions may be placed on its use. There are no age limits.

### Permits and Licenses in General

Forms for application for Restricted Operator Permits and Ship Station License are usually packed with sets when they are shipped from the manufacturer, but the new FCC Form 155 may not be included. If you need application forms at a time other than when purchasing a new set, you probably can get them from a marine radio dealer. If you encounter problems, write to your regional FCC office.

Each higher grade of operator license includes all privileges of any lower grade; if you have a Marine Radio Operator Permit, for instance, it is not necessary to also have a Restricted Permit.

### Restricted Radiotelephone Operator Permit

The lowest grade—Restricted Radiotelephone Operator Permit—is what you must have if you are going to operate your VHF radio outside U.S. territorial waters (now the 12-mile limit) or in the waters of another country. It is also required if you intend to equip your boat with an SSB radio and use it on the MF and HF bands.

You obtain a Restricted Permit by filling out FCC Form 753 and mailing it to the Federal Communications Commission, Restricted Permit, P.O. Box 358295, Pittsburgh, PA 15251-5295. The fee is $35, and this amount plus FCC Form 155 must accompany the application; the Fee Type Code is "PAR."

There is no examination. The permit is issued on your certification that (1) you can speak and hear; (2) you can keep a rough written log; and (3) you are familiar with the provisions of applicable treaties, laws, rules, and regulations. You also must certify that you are eligible for employment in the United States (all citizens and some others), and that you need the permit because you intend to engage in international voyages. The FCC Rules do not require a radio operator permit for the use of a marine VHF transmitter in U.S. waters on vessels that are voluntarily equipped. The regulations do, however, require at least the Restricted Permit if you will be cruising to or from ports in foreign countries, including Mexico and Canada. The Restricted Permit is also required for the operation of MF/HF SSB sets in *all* waters. The application ends with your signature beneath a certification that all statements made on the form are "true to the best of your knowledge." False statements are a federal criminal offense.

FCC Form 753 has three parts. You complete all three parts, but mail in only two—the upper portion, which is the application form, and the middle section, which will be mailed back to you as your permit. You retain the lower portion of the form to serve as your Temporary Permit pending receipt back from the FCC of the permit itself. This allows you to get on the air immediately and is valid for 60 days from the date on which you mailed your application to the FCC.

If you are not a U.S. citizen, *and* you are not eligible for employment in the United States, but you need the Restricted Permit because you hold a station license and need a permit to operate that station, you may still be able to obtain a permit limited to that station only. Application must be made on FCC Form 755. The same fee, fee submission form, and procedures described above are used.

A holder of the Restricted Permit is not authorized to make any equipment adjustments that might affect transmitter operations, nor to operate any transmitter that requires the use of other than simple switches for frequency selection; the frequency of the transmitter must be controlled from within the unit.

The reverse sides of both the temporary and the regular Restricted Permits carry information about certain actions that are illegal in the operation of a radio transmitter. You should read and carefully observe these limitations and prohibitions.

The Restricted Radiotelephone Operator Permit is good for life and you never need to renew it. The Restricted Permit must be carried on your person, or posted on your boat whenever you are operating your radio under circumstances in which it is required.

### Marine Radio Operator Permit

The next step up the ladder of FCC radio licenses is the Marine Radio Operator Permit. The regulations require this permit on craft that are compulsorily equipped with radios, such as boats for hire carrying more than six persons. (Such small passenger-vessels are exempted from the requirement to have a VHF radio if they are under 50 gross tons and do not operate more than 1,000 feet from shore at mean low tide.)

Marine Radio Operator Permits must be applied for in person at an FCC field office. A written examination is required. This test is not technical, but merely covers major points in the rules and regulations, as well as basic operating procedures and practices. With preparation, it should not be difficult to pass. The passing grade is 75 percent; a failed exam may be retaken after 60 days.

The request for examination is made on FCC Form 756. Form 155 must also be completed; the FCC office where the examination is to be taken can advise you of the correct Fee Type Code. The fee for the Marine Radio Operator Permit examination is $35; the fee must be paid again if the examination is retaken.

The Marine Operator Permit is issued for a term of five years, and it must be renewed. This can be done at any time in the last year of the term. There are no service or examination requirements for renewal. The request for renewal is made on Form 756, and a fee of $35 must be included together with a FCC Form 155. If you miss your renewal date, the permit can be renewed during a five-year grace period, but it is not *valid for use* during that period. If the grace period has expired, you must apply for a new permit and take an examination.

### General Radiotelephone Operator License

This is the highest grade of radiotelephone license (there is a separate series of licenses for radiotelegraph operators). It is the license that the FCC requires for anyone who does technical servicing on VHF or SSB transmitters and transceivers used on boats. It is also required for the operation of radio stations on compulsorily equipped large ships and higher-powered stations on land.

The examination for this license covers both regulatory and technical topics to ensure that holders are competent to do maintenance work and to operate higher-powered stations that might cause interference over wide areas. The passing grade is 75 percent; failed tests may be retaken after a waiting period of 60 days. The fee for this license examination is $35, and the procedures are the same as those for the Marine Radio Operator Permit. The General Operator License is valid for the lifetime of the holder and need not be renewed.

## Radio Station Licenses

All marine radio stations on ships—and remember that recreational vessels are "ships" in the eyes of the FCC—must be licensed. (CB sets, even on boats, do not require a license.) The license refers only to the transmitter portion of the equipment. No license is required to use a receiver only on board, or for any device that does not send out a signal, like a radio direction finder, loran, satellite, or other navigational receiver. A license is required for a radar.

Station licenses provide both the authority to operate a transmitter and the call letters that you will use to identify your station on the air.

### Application for Ship Station License

Ship Station Licenses can be applied for by mail using FCC Form 506. You must have state registration numbers, or a Coast Guard documentation number, for your boat before you apply. Like the application for a Restricted Operator Permit, this is a multipart form that allows you to retain a portion as a temporary license pending receipt of the formal license from the FCC; the temporary permit is valid for 90 days. Detailed instructions for completion of the application appear on the first two pages of the form. Read and follow these carefully to avoid having your application returned for correction or additional information. The following two-page sheet is the actual application that will be mailed to the FCC. A fee of $35 and FCC Form 155 must accompany the application; the Fee Type Code is "PAS." Mail these papers to the Federal Communications Commission, Marine Ship Service, Pittsburgh, P.O. Box 358275, Pittsburgh, PA 15251-5275.

The final two-page sheet of paper becomes Form 506A, a temporary license. It provides information for generating a temporary call sign that can be used until the regular call sign is received on the formal station license. For boats registered by state authorities, the temporary call sign is the letter K followed by the state registration numbers. For example, a boat with the state registration numbers FL 5427 GJ would be identified on the air as KFL 5427 GJ. A vessel documented by the Coast Guard gets a temporary call sign by adding the letters KUS before the Official Number that appears on the Certificate of Documentation. For example, a boat with the documentation number 910390 would use the temporary call sign KUS 910390. *The use of such a temporary call sign must cease as soon as you receive the regular license and call letters*, even if the 90-day period has not expired.

Ship Station Licenses authorize the use of certain, specified frequency bands. The application form includes boxes to be checked to indicate the frequency bands that you will need for the various types of equipment that you expect to use. Plan ahead; check boxes even if you do not yet have the equipment. The use of SSB equipment for the MF and HF bands will be authorized only for vessels to be also equipped with VHF sets. Class A and B EPIRB operation will be authorized only for vessels expected to travel in waters beyond normal marine VHF range, assumed in the regulations to be 37 km (20 miles) offshore. The same restriction will apply to the newer category 1 and 2 EPIRBs.

## Modification and Renewal

A Ship Station License may need to be modified under certain circumstances. If it becomes necessary to use frequency bands not covered by the original license—say, after the addition of SSB equipment—a new FCC Form 506 must be submitted, indicating in Item 5 that the application is for a modification of the license. A fee of $35 and FCC Form 155 are required; the Fee Type Code is "PAS." Mere replacement of one set by another, with no change in the frequencies used, does not require modification of the station license.

A change in the name of the vessel or a change in the mailing address of the licensee must be reported to the FCC, Gettysburg, PA. The use of FCC Form 405-A or a letter is sufficient; no fee is required. A copy of the form or letter must be kept with the license. A license cannot be transferred from one boat to another. A change of vessel requires application for a new license, even if you move the same equipment over to the new boat.

The Ship Station License term is for five years, and application for renewal without modification must be made on FCC Form 405-B. The application for renewal should be made 120 days before the expiration of the license term. The FCC is supposed to send Form 405-B to you automatically. If you do not receive it, you can use Form 506 for renewal, marking the appropriate box in Item 5. If a modification of the license is desired at the time of renewal, a Form 506 must be used instead of Form 405-B. A fee of $35 and Form 155 must also accompany this application for renewal; the Fee Type Code is "PAS." The address to be used is Federal Communications Commission, 405-B Station Renewal, P.O. Box 358290, Pittsburgh, PA 15251-5290.

If you have not received a renewed license before the expiration date of the old one, you may continue to operate as long as you have applied for renewal. You do not need to have a temporary authorization, but you must keep a copy of the renewal application with your old station license. If you do not make a timely application for renewal, you must stop using your set until you do have an effective license.

## Termination of Use

An FCC station license for a vessel is not transferable. If you sell your boat, return the license to the FCC for cancellation. If you do not do this, you are legally liable for any misuse of the station by the new owner. It is also advisable to have the license canceled if the boat sinks or is otherwise removed from use. If for some reason the station license is not available, write to the FCC, explaining why the license cannot be sent in and requesting cancellation.

## Licenses for Hand-Held Sets

You may use a hand-held set as your main radio on a boat; it must be licensed in the same manner as if it were an installed transceiver.

A hand-held set also can be used as an **associated ship unit**, in which case it can be in limited use off the boat but is not separately licensed (see Chapter 5). If your dinghy is a registered boat with state numbers, you can have a station license for it and use the hand-held set as the boat's radio under the same operating rules as apply to the installed set on the parent vessel.

## Permits and Licenses in General

Each higher grade of operator license includes all privileges of any lower grade—if you have a Marine Radio Operator Permit, it is not necessary also to have a Restricted Permit for use under conditions where such are needed.

If a license or permit is lost or so damaged as to be illegible, you must file an application for replacement, including a written explanation of the circumstances involved. A signed copy of the application must be posted or carried until the replacement is received.

# CHAPTER FOUR

# VHF RADIO EQUIPMENT AND OPERATION

Setting up VHF radio on your boat is so simple that many recreational mariners install the gear themselves. The most difficult task you will have is to choose the gear that will do the best job for you out of the many excellent pieces of equipment available today. The heart of the system is the *transceiver*, a surprisingly small unit that combines the transmitter and the receiver. This makes for a compact and economical package that can be installed on any small boat, as the major electronic elements can share some components and circuits. A microphone and a speaker or speakers come with the set. The other component you will need in order to get on the air and to broadcast clearly is an antenna. These vary in type and range. An adjunct to your VHF gear, or perhaps used as your basic unit, is a portable hand-held transceiver, which can be used in small, open boats of all types, even dinghies.

## Selecting a Transceiver

When shopping for a transceiver, you will note that the unit is "Type Accepted," an FCC requirement that keeps poor products off the airwaves. This should pose no problem in the selection of a unit, for all sets sold must meet the FCC's stringent criteria. Occasionally, manufacturers will advertise a model with the notation, "FCC Type Acceptance Pending." Make sure acceptance has been granted before buying. Try to find someone with a transceiver of the type you are looking for, and ask the person how satisfied he or she is with the transceiver and dealer service.

Prices for VHF marine transceivers range from $150 to $900 or more; there is a set for every budget. As marine radiotelephone is a requisite for safety, you should get as good a set as you can afford. A higher cost means better construction and reliability plus special features.

Receivers, however, are not standardized by the government and here is where you will find the biggest differences in quality. Among the characteristics to look for are *sensitivity*—the ability of the receiver to hear weak signals—and *selectivity*—rejection of adjacent channel frequencies. Also look for LCD (liquid crystal display) read-outs of the channel numbers (they are easier to see in bright sunshine) and good audio power (Can you hear the speaker over the noise of the engine?).

But first, one practical consideration—plan your installation before you make any decision as to which set to purchase. Where you want to place the transceiver on your boat may affect how large or small a unit you buy, and whether a "reversible front panel" is necessary.

Below is a discussion of some other criteria to help you choose a transceiver.

## Number of Channels

As opposed to early sets with individual crystals for each frequency (usually up to 12), today's VHF transceivers use "frequency synthesizers," which provide 55 basic channels and up. Fifty-five is all you will ever need in the United States and Canada. There is still a requirement in the regulations that you have Channel 16, Channel 06, and one working channel on your set; with a synthesized transceiver you will have all of the authorized working channels available to you.

Don't be misled by the number of channels advertised for various VHF sets; you may see claims of more than 100. The designs and methods of counting channels vary among manufacturers. All transceivers, except for a very few hand-held models, will have all the channels you can legally use, whether you are engaged in commercial or noncommercial operations. You will occasionally see advertisements for more expensive VHFs claiming that the sets are capable of operating on the "expansion" channels when such are authorized. The FCC has formally announced that there are no plans for expanding the channels in the VHF marine band and that such capability is of little value.

Channel selection may be made by a rotary knob or on a key pad (like those of a touch-tone phone or a calculator). Transceivers with key pads tend to have more associated functions besides channel selection. They usually have a membrane under the key pad to keep moisture from getting to the components. Rotary knob units are simpler and easier to work with gloved hands, but the channel selector contacts may be subject to corrosion. Hand-held VHFs may use either of these methods or a pair of thumbwheel switches.

## Output Power

Twenty-five watts is the maximum legal output power for a VHF ship station transceiver; hand-helds run about 3 to 6 watts. In addition, all transceivers must be able to switch to the low-power transmission of 1 watt, which is mandated for use on the Bridge-to-Bridge channels, 13 and 67. Use low power also in harbor, for conversation with nearby vessels and shore stations. Use full power for calling the Coast Guard, for emergency situations on Channels 16 and 06, and for communicating with vessels and shore some distance away. Transceivers manufactured under recent regulations must have built-in circuitry that switches to 1 watt output when Channel 13 or 67 is selected. Hand-held sets have a manual switch to go to low power.

## Special Features

Since VHF transceivers are typecast by federal regulation and are pretty much alike inside, and also have the same channel capability, your specific choice will probably be influenced by the special features that come with it. These may add to the cost of a set, but they can be very useful and convenient assets. They include:

*Memory Channels:* From a few to as many as 48, the most often used channels can be stored in a memory bank and then quickly called upon when needed.

*Dual Watch (Sequential Dual Channel Reception):* This feature allows you to maintain a watch on Channel 16 while simultaneously monitoring another channel of your choice, such as the working channel being used by your cruising group. The set basically stays on the working channel but every few seconds switches to 16 for a brief moment. If it detects no signal it stays on the working channel; otherwise it stays on Channel 16. (Note, however, that sequential dual channel reception is not acceptable for a watch required by the Great Lakes Radio Agreement or the Bridge-to-Bridge Radio Act.)

*Scanning:* With this special feature you can set up the receiver to listen sequentially to all channels except ones you have "locked out," or to channels in the receiver's memory. When the set is scanning, it proceeds rapidly across the silent channels and stops on one that is in use. The scanner can be programmed to stay on the channel or to resume scanning after a pause of a few seconds. The scanner will always revert to Channel 16 when a signal is picked up there.

*Weather Alert:* This feature enables your system to maintain a silent watch on a selected weather channel. If an NOAA weather station transmits the tone warning signal that precedes all weather alerts, the set automatically switches to the weather channel so that you get the warning immediately.

*Reversible Front Panel:* This is often desirable because it permits a greater flexibility in the mounting of the unit—horizontally on a shelf or into a bulkhead or overhead, or vertically on a bulkhead. Other options that are useful when installing VHF include a *remote speaker*, which allows a watch to be kept elsewhere than at the set itself. On some sets this remote speaker can serve as an intercom station or even as a loud-hailer. Even more flexible is a two-unit package in which the transceiver can be located out of the way in a convenient place and the set operated and controlled by telephone-like handsets at the control or navigation stations.

### Special Features of Hand-helds

Small hand-held transceivers can have many of the special features of installed sets—memory channels, dual watch, and scanning—as well as other features that are specific to these portable units. A power-save mode will extend battery life by reducing drainage during periods of inactivity even though the set is left on. Some models have slide-on batteries that permit you to carry a spare charged battery, making the switch quickly and easily without opening the case of the set (thus keeping the contacts clean and bright). You should have two chargers, one that operates from 12-V DC sources and another that operates from 120-V AC sources. This will enable you to charge your hand-held's battery regardless of which primary power source is available.

A most important accessory for a hand-held transceiver is a waterproof bag—electronic equipment and water, especially salt water, are not compatible. A plastic freezer-bag can be used for transporting the set in a dinghy or other small boat, but much better is a heavy-duty plastic bag shaped to hold the set with its antenna on it in such a position that it can be operated without being removed from the bag.

## Selecting a VHF Antenna for a Small Boat

Besides selecting a set, you also must choose an antenna. The choice of an antenna involves the size and "gain" of the specific unit; these are interrelated factors. The proper location of the antenna on your boat is also important and may influence your selection. If yours is a sailboat installation and you choose to put the antenna at the mast-head, you also will have to make a decision about the type of coaxial cable to use. The following basic information will help you make an informed selection.

### Antenna Fundamentals

Marine antennas are made so that they radiate signals equally in all horizontal directions but not straight up. Since an upward signal in the VHF range is not reflected back and is therefore wasted, the objective is to reduce upward radiation in a VHF antenna and enhance the signal beamed toward the horizon. The degree to which this is accomplished is called the antenna's "gain." It is measured in decibels (dB)

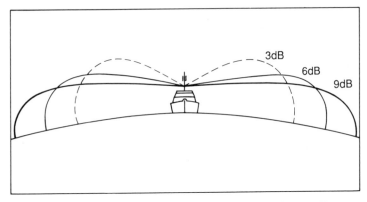

*Figure 4.1 A higher gain antenna produces greater range for a VHF trans-mitter by "squeezing down" the radiated power so that more of it flows out close to the water's surface, where it is effective. Less power is wasted in higher-angle radiation that never reaches another station.*

and is one of the major factors in choosing an antenna. In terms of effective radiated power (ERP), antennas are rated on the basis of how much gain they have over a theoretical antenna with zero gain. A 3-foot, 3-dB antenna represents twice as much gain over the imaginary antenna, a 9-foot, 6-dB antenna a four-fold increase, and a 23-foot, 9-dB antenna an even greater increase. You can see, then, how the char-acteristics of an antenna system (it has a built-in ground) affect the distance you can hear and be heard. The length of the antenna you choose, however, must also be related to the size of your boat. As an extreme example, a 9-dB antenna (19 to 23 feet) would be suitable for a 60-foot sportfisherman, but out of place on a 23-foot center fishing boat. What you are looking for in an antenna is range; the most expen-sive VHF transceiver on the market will not get a proper signal to the horizon and just a little bit beyond without the proper antenna matchup of height above the water and appropriate gain.

Sailboats usually achieve that goal with a 36-to 42-inch, 3-dB stainless steel "whip" antenna mounted on the masthead. A favorite for smaller powerboats is the 9-foot, 6-dB fiberglass antenna.

## Coaxial Cable

VHF antennas are connected to the transceiver by means of a coaxial cable—a shielded transmission line with a sleeve like configuration in which an inner conducting wire runs through PVC insulation, which is in turn surrounded by a braided wire shield that also acts as a conductor. The outer skin of the cable is a heavy vinyl jacket that preserves its conductivity and keeps the conductors dry. Coaxial cable is especially meant for radio transmission. Because of a phenomenon called "skin effect," frequency current is carried on the outside of the inner wire and on the inside of the shield, so the packaging is very important in limiting the loss of power between the transmitter and the antenna. The larger the diameter of the cable and the better the quality of the insulation around the conducting wire in the center, the less will be the loss. The actual loss is determined by the length; loss is stated as "dB per 100 feet." If the loss were as great as 3 dB, then only half the power of the transceiver would reach the antenna.

Coaxial cable is designated by the prefix RG (Radio Government) and is specified by its diameter and construction. For runs of less than 20 feet, RG-8/U, about 1/4 inch diameter, is a good choice. For runs over 20 feet, the larger (and more expensive) RG-213/U is a waterproof, abrasion and ultraviolet resistant cable that should provide many years of service. At 156.8 MHz, a 100-foot run will have about 2.3-dB loss.

Be wise and careful in purchasing coax cable. Buy from qualified marine-radio dealers. Do not use coaxial cable meant for CB installations, as it tends to lose radio frequency power because of the way it is constructed. You cannot substitute TV cable either, for it will not match the requirements of your transceiver or antenna.

# Installation

Installation of your VHF radio is not complicated. If you use a few simple tools, the job can be done in an hour or two. The whole task consists of physically mounting the transceiver in a convenient location where it and the microphone are accessible to the helmsperson

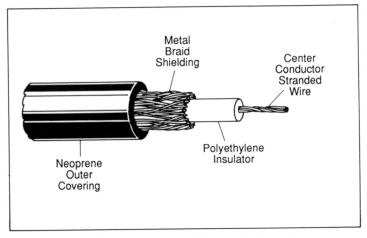

*Figure 4.2  Coaxial cable—commonly called "coax"—is used to connect a VHF set to its antenna. It is available in many types; be sure to use the correct type for your installation.*

and crew, mounting the antenna, connecting the antenna cable, and running power leads from your 12-volt battery.

**Installing the Transceiver**

When selecting the set, it is useful to keep in mind where it will be located on the boat and even to take measurements of the unit and speaker (if the speaker is separate) to check that they will fit. Make sure the speaker can be heard by the person at the helm, especially over the noise of engines running at high RPM. Because of the strong magnet in the speaker, the transceiver should be located at least 3 feet from the boat's compass. The microphone and its holder are nonmagnetic and can be closer. The bracket that holds the transceiver should be firmly mounted on any surface that provides the necessary separation from the compass and convenience to the skipper. Power leads may run directly to the battery or to a distribution panel, where a fuse or circuit breaker can protect from short-circuits. This also provides a means of shutting off power to the set when it is being installed or removed.

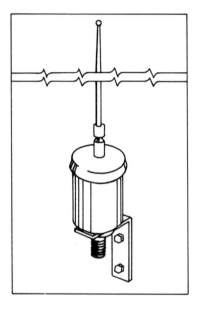

*Figure 4.3 An effective antenna for the top of a sailboat or trawler mast is a "base-loaded" whip. The antenna is at ground potential for DC and can provide lightning protection, which a fiberglass whip cannot.*

**Installing the Antenna and the Cable**

On a powerboat, the base fitting for the antenna must be located on a strong and firm surface; it should be as high as is practicable. Use through-bolts if possible, or otherwise self-taping screws of adequate size. Bedding compound should be applied liberally under the base, and especially around the holes through the surface on which it is mounted. If possible, avoid running the antenna cable through a horizontal surface, such as a cabin top. If you run the coax through a side panel, use a waterproof fitting and provide a "drip loop" just before the cable enters the fitting (see Figure 4.4). Make sure, also, that there is sufficient slack in the coax so the antenna can be sloped back or laid down flat, backward or forward, if it is necessary to reduce the vertical clearance requirement of your boat for a bridge or covered storage shed.

A possible difficulty arises here. The watertight fitting is designed to be just large enough for the coax cable, usually the smaller RG-

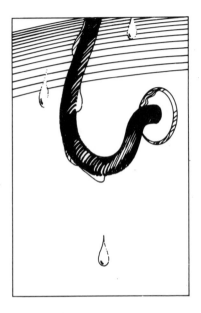

*Figure 4.4  Where a coax cable antenna lead-in must come through the side of your boat's cabin , use a watertight fitting and provide a "drip loop" to prevent water from collecting at the fitting.*

58/U type, but is not large enough to pass the PL-259 connector that normally comes on the end of an attached antenna cable. Thus, you will have to cut off this plug and reattach it after feeding the cable through the fitting. At the same time, you can shorten the cable to eliminate any unnecessary slack. Reattaching the connector requires a bit of soldering skill, but it can be done properly if you follow the instructions that come with the connector and take care to do a good job. Do *not* use a "solderless" connector in a marine environment—corrosion will soon result in a poor connection. Dimensions for cutting back the outer covering, braid, and inner insulation are shown in Figure 4.5. The larger RG-8/U and similar size coax use a PL-259 (83-1SP) connector directly. For the smaller RG 58/U coax, you will need an 83-168 adapter.

If you have a sailboat, you will need to make a choice of antenna location before purchasing your equipment. A masthead location provides height, but use of a masthead antenna is lost in a dismasting, just when the radio is most needed to summon assistance. A mount clamped to the rail near the stern is a possible alter-

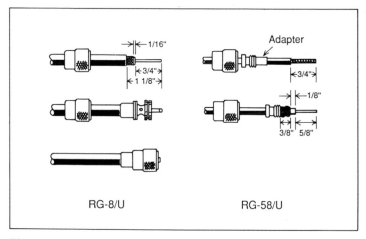

*Figure 4.5 To get your coax cable through a fitting and into your boat's interior, you may have to cut off the end plug and reattach it later. You can do this if you follow the directions that come with the connector. Be sure to make good soldered connections.*

native to a masthead for an antenna, or it could be a location for an emergency antenna that would be used only when the masthead antenna is no longer functional.

If your antenna is at the masthead, the coax cable will have to be run down inside the mast, and here you may need the help of skilled personnel at a boatyard. If you choose a lower mounting location such as the rail near the stern, the installation is essentially the same as for a powerboat, with a relatively short run of cable to the set.

Regardless of your type of antenna, it is desirable to check its operation after installation. If you have, or can borrow, a suitable SWR (Standing Wave Ratio) meter, put it between the transceiver antenna connection and the coax cable. This must be a meter intended for use at marine VHF frequencies; a meter sold for use with CB sets cannot be relied upon for accurate readings. A perfect antenna would show an SWR of 1:1, but do not expect this from a typical boat installation. A reading of 1.5:1 is desirable, but 2:1 is acceptable; the lower the better is the rule. If your SWR reading is too high, look first for bad connections between your coax line and its fittings, or see if your antenna is too close to other metal objects. Make a record of the SWR reading at the time of installation so that it can be compared with later readings to find any deterioration in performance.

A ground connection (needed in SSB) is not required for a VHF antenna.

## Maintenance

Marine VHF radios, even the less expensive units, are generally well constructed, and trouble is very infrequent. If the set fails to switch on, check any fuse or circuit breaker in the power lead; if these are o.k., then it's a job for an electronics shop. If the fuse or circuit breaker is blown, replace it (or turn on the breaker), but if it blows a second time, turn off the set and take it to a shop.

If the set does switch on, but you are unable to contact anyone, the problem could lie in the transceiver, or it could be in the antenna. You can save yourself time and money by determining which is at fault before calling in technical assistance. If possible, try your set with the antenna of another boat, and try another set on your antenna. This should reveal which is the defective element, and eliminate the one that is satisfactory. Remove only the defective unit and take it to the shop.

### Retuning

After several years on your boat, it is possible that the tuned circuits in the transceiver may have aged and gotten a bit out of adjustment. If you receive reports of noise on your signals or a fuzziness to your voice, your set is probably slightly off frequency. Similarly, if you notice a loss of sensitivity in your reception of other signals, your set is probably getting out of tune. (Make sure that you are using the squelch control properly. Too high a setting will keep you from hearing weaker signals; check the instruction manual that came with the set.) Both because you want to have efficient communications and to avoid a citation from the FCC for off-frequency operation, you should take your set to a marine electronics repair shop for periodic retuning.

**Antenna Maintenance**

If you have, or can borrow, an SWR meter, you should check your antenna system whenever you have reason to suspect trouble there. A reading of 1.5 or less is desirable; in any case, compare the current reading with that taken at the time of installation. You cannot check a VHF antenna with an ordinary ohmmeter; designs vary and you may get an indication of either a shorted or open circuit, both of which are meaningless in this instance.

Over a period of years, your fiberglass antenna may show signs of aging in the form of shredding on the surface. This will not affect its operation as an antenna, but its appearance can be restored by applying a coat of resin or varnish.

You should not hear a rattle when you shake your antenna. If you do, it means that supporting insulators inside have deteriorated and/or may be loose. Make an SWR check, and replace the antenna if the reading is greater than acceptable. An annual SWR check is good practice even if you do not have any reason to suspect problems; some deterioration is so slow as to escape detection in routine operation.

# OPERATING YOUR VHF RADIO

The cardinal principle in transmitting on any marine VHF radio is brevity! Always remember that only one station can effectively transmit at any given time. Courtesy on the air must be the guiding principle; *always listen on a channel before you transmit* (an FCC regulation). Frequency modulated (FM) transmissions have a special characteristic called the "capture effect." If two stations are transmitting at the same time, they do not actually interfere with each other, but rather the stronger signal "captures" the channel and is heard, while the other signal, or signals, are completely blocked out. (When yours are the overridden signals, the colloquial term is that you have been

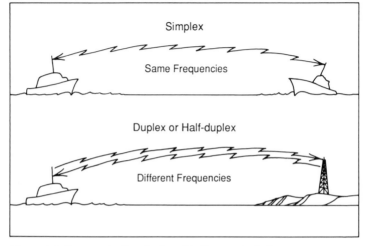

*Figure 4.6  Communications back and forth on a single frequency are termed "simplex." The use of two frequencies is called "duplex" if both stations can transmit at the same time, "half-duplex" if they must transmit alternately (as in simplex).*

"stepped on.") Always use the minimum power required to carry on your communications (use the "1-watt" or "low power" setting on your radio whenever possible).

Technical terms for types of radio operation include "simplex," "full-duplex," and "half-duplex." Briefly, in simplex communications both stations use the same frequency, with each station transmitting and receiving alternately. In full-duplex operation, each station transmits on its own frequency and receives on the other station's transmitting frequency even while it is transmitting. In half-duplex, two frequencies are used, but the station that is transmitting on one frequency is not simultaneously receiving on the other. All VHF marine radio communications are simplex, except contacts with a public coast station ("Marine Operator"), which are half-duplex. In both cases, when you are talking you cannot be interrupted. You will not hear the other person until you let up on the switch on your microphone, your "mike button."

## Mandatory Listening Watches

For various types and sizes of vessels in various operating situations, the FCC prescribes mandatory listening watches. These are mostly on Channel 16, but some are on 13 and 67. The skipper of every radio-equipped vessel must know the circumstances under which he or she is required to maintain an effective listening watch on one or more channels. The purpose of mandatory watches is to ensure that a vessel can be contacted for safety and navigational communications when needed. They also provide a known channel for calling another station. (Imagine the confusion and additional transmissions if you had to try many different channels to find the party to whom you wished to talk!)

*Recreational boats are not required to have their radios on, but if they are on, and not being actively used for communications on another frequency, they must be tuned to Channel 16 and an effective watch must be maintained .*

The current drain of a VHF transceiver while receiving is very slight—roughly half an ampere. This is not great enough to cause concern over running down a battery by keeping a listening watch while your boat is at anchor or under sail.

Since commercial craft carrying six or fewer passengers for hire are considered voluntarily equipped, they are subject to the provisions noted above for noncommercial boats. And, as mentioned in Chapter 1, craft for hire carrying more than six passengers must have a radio. As a compulsorily equipped vessel, such a boat must keep its radio turned on for a mandatory watch. The radio must be tuned to VHF Channel 16 for inland and coastal operations. When beyond the service area of a VHF coast station, such vessels also must keep a watch on 2182 kHz, SSB. See Chapter 2 for other mandatory watch regulations.

# GENERAL COMMUNICATION PROCEDURES

**Who May Use Your Radio**

A radio operator permit is not required in order to use a VHF radio in U.S. waters. Outside these waters, and for other frequency bands in all waters, you must have a Restricted Radiotelephone Operator Permit or higher-grade license. However, an unlicensed individual may talk over the radio provided that a properly licensed individual is present and supervises the use of the transmitter. The licensed individual should establish the contact with the other station and begin and conclude the contact with the calling station's identification.

**Station Identification**

*When Station Identification is Required:* The FCC regulations require that radio transmissions be identified at specified events and intervals. Call-sign identification is required of a boat radio station at the beginning and end of each communication with another station. Note that while this identification is required when calling another station on Channel 16, it is *not* required for the initial call on the working channel after shifting from 16. Do not add to the length of your transmissions by giving your call letters when they are not required. Give your call sign again when ending your contact with the other station. Identification is also required at fifteen-minute intervals should transmissions continue for more than that length of time; but this would be exceedingly rare. You can give your call sign at other, additional, times, but this is generally not desirable—remember, "brevity" is our watchword!

Identification by call letters is not required when operating on a Bridge-to-Bridge channel, such as 13 or 67.

*How Identification is Given:* Call-sign identification is made by simply stating the letters and digits. It is required that the call sign be given in the English language, but the letters need not be stated in the phonetic alphabet. Phonetics are essential, however, in important communications, such as with the Coast Guard in an emergency to

## Standard Phonetic Spelling Alphabet

| | | | |
|---|---|---|---|
| **A** | ALFA | **N** | NOVEMBER |
| **B** | BRAVO | **O** | OSCAR |
| **C** | CHARLIE | **P** | PAPA |
| **D** | DELTA | **Q** | QUEBEC |
| **E** | ECHO | **R** | ROMEO |
| **F** | FOXTROT | **S** | SIERRA |
| **G** | GOLF | **T** | TANGO |
| **H** | HOTEL | **U** | UNIFORM |
| **I** | INDIA | **V** | VICTOR |
| **J** | JULIETT | **W** | WHISKEY |
| **K** | KILO | **X** | X-RAY |
| **L** | LIMA | **Y** | YANKEE |
| **M** | MIKE | **Z** | ZULU |

*Figure 4.7 Many letters, when spoken individually, sound much the same, especially over the radio. The use of phonetic equivalents will prevent misunderstanding and possible confusion, but don't overuse them. When needed, you should use the internationally accepted Phonetic Alphabet shown above rather than one you make up yourself.*

confirm the identity of the station. If you do use phonetics, use the standardized alphabet for the sake of clarity and quick understanding. Do not use words that you have made up yourself. While inclusion of the vessel's name in your identification is not required, few people would recognize who was calling from the FCC call letters alone, so that in actual practice the name is always used.

*The International Phonetic Alphabet:* Many letters of the alphabet sound somewhat alike, especially over a radio circuit, which is subject to noise, distortion, and fading. For example, the letters "B," "C," "D," "E," "G," "P," and "T"; "M" and "N"; and even "A," "J," and "K," respectively, have a somewhat similar sound and are subject to confusion. The possibilities of being misunderstood are compounded when the person with whom you are communicating is not English-speaking. To insure proper and rapid comprehension, an alphabet of phonetic equivalent words has been established internationally (see Figure 4.7). It is used by military and naval forces, commercial and private aviators, and many others worldwide. It is well worth the short time that it would take you to learn it, and regular use will soon make it second nature to you. Phonetics can be essential, not only with call signs, but also in spelling out your name, the name of your vessel, place names, and many other words that may not be familiar to the person on the other end of the radio conversation.

**Procedure Words**

Properly used, *procedure words* can reduce the length of transmissions, conveying one or more complete thoughts through a single word or two. The words "over" and "out" are all-too-often misused as synonyms; they have specific and contradictory meanings and should never be combined.

*Over:* This procedure word is used at the end of a transmission. It means that you have finished this particular transmission and will now listen for a reply from the other station. Use "Over" sparingly; limit it to conversations with persons not familiar with radio communications, or to times when receiving conditions are marginal.

*Out:* This procedure word is also used at the end of a transmission, but only at the end of the *last* transmission of a specific contact with another station. It means that you have finished your transmission and are *not* requesting or expecting a reply. Its use is not really necessary. If you conclude with your station call sign, as you must, it is an obvious indication that the contact is concluded. (The word *Clear* is sometimes used at the end of a contact; this is nonstandard but readily understood.)

*Roger:* This is another communications procedure word that has become universally accepted. (At one time it was the phonetic equivalent for the letter *R*, which is used in radiotelegraphy to mean "Received.") Specifically, it means that you have received *and understood* the other station's last transmission. Do *not* use it if reception and understanding are less than *full and complete*; to say "Roger, except for . . ." is poor procedure. *Wilco* has the same meaning, along with your statement that you will comply with whatever the request or instruction was.

*Say Again:* This phrase is used to request a repetition of all or a part of a transmission. It is also used to identify a repetition that you are making, as in "I Say Again." This is preferable to using "Repeat".

*This is:* These are the procedure words that precede the name and/or call sign of the transmitting station to identify it when calling or communicating with another station.

*Affirmative:* This procedure word can have several meanings, including "You are correct" and, simply, "Yes." *Negative* has the opposite meaning.

*Wait:* This procedure word is used to indicate that you must pause, but want the other station to continue to listen for you rather than reply. It can be made more specific by adding a number— for example, "Wait One," meaning that the pause will be about one minute in duration.

*Break:* This procedure word can be useful if you are communicating with more than one station at a time and wish to mark a change in your transmission from one station to another; it also can be used to indicate the separation between formal messages if you are transmitting more than one in a row.

*I Spell:* Although not absolutely necessary, this is often a useful indicator used after a word you have spoken to show that what follows are the phonetic letters of that word. For example: "Shape—I Spell—Sierra, Hotel, Alpha, Papa, Echo."

**Intership Communications**

Remember that intership is the term that the FCC uses for communications between vessels of all sizes. As noted earlier, the range over which boat-to-boat VHF contacts may be made will largely be determined by the height of the respective antennas, and to a lesser degree by the type of antenna (3 dB, 6 dB). Sailboats with masthead antennas have a definite advantage here. Consistent ranges of 10 to 15 miles can be expected between powerboats with 6-dB antennas 6 feet or so above the water. A sailboat with a 3-dB masthead antenna might reach out to 20 miles or a bit more to a similar craft. Ranges between a sailboat and a powerboat would fall somewhere between these distances. There is nothing absolute about these ranges, and variations must always be expected. They are for over-water communications; intervening land masses will reduce the distance somewhat, but not predictably. Occasional atmospheric conditions will result in "ducting," when the higher-angle VHF signals that normally escape are trapped and forced around the earth's surface beyond the normal radio horizon, resulting in transmissions that are heard at abnormally great distances, sometimes as far as several hundred miles.

**Establishing Contact**

When you wish to establish communications with another boat, call on Channel 16 unless you are certain that the other skipper is also listening on another channel that is known to you. There is no legally required procedure to be used, but there is one that long experience has shown to be most effective. Press your mike button and make the call as follows:

*(The name of the other vessel)*

*This is (the name of your vessel and your call sign)*

*The procedure word "Over" can be spoken here, but is normally unnecessary.*

This sequence of words is far better than first stating your boat's name, then "calling," followed by the other craft's name. What gets the other skipper's attention is his or her boat's name. If you give your craft's name first, the other skipper may well have been paying no attention at that moment, and several additional transmissions will be required to straighten out who is calling him or her. Do not forget that you must give your call sign as part of the initial call, and that you ought to give your boat's name, too.

There are time limitations when you call another station. No one transmission can last longer than 30 seconds; normally it is very much less. State the name of the vessel only once unless receiving conditions are bad. If necessary, give the name two or three times, but no more; give the call sign only once. If the called station does not respond, you must wait for two minutes before calling again. After three calls, you must stop calling and wait for fifteen minutes

## "Trident
## This is
## Leeway, WTC 5074
## Over"

*Figure 4.8 It is important to use the proper sequence of items when calling another boat or radio station. If the sequence is inverted, it is likely that additional transmissions will be needed to establish contact. Rarely is it necessary to speak both boat names more than once.*

before starting another series of calls, again spaced two minutes apart, *unless* "there is no reason to believe that harmful interference will be caused to other communications in progress; in this case," the fifteen-minute delay can be reduced to three minutes. These limitations do not, of course, apply in emergencies.

Once you make contact, the next action is to immediately establish which "working channel" will be used for conversing. Do not use Channel 16 for even the briefest of messages! If the signals are loud and clear, the called station can immediately answer with a working channel, thus saving one or more transmissions. The station to which a working channel is proposed should always confirm the number of that channel. The FCC requires that the exchange of transmissions on Channel 16 not exceed one minute in duration.

If you are sure that the other skipper is listening simultaneously to both 16 and a working channel, call him or her directly on the working channel. Or, if you have recently had a good contact with the other station, you can propose the working channel (preferably the one that you have been using to communicate with that station) by including in your initial call on 16 the statement "Switch and answer Channel ___," and then switch immediately to that channel.

### Talking with Another Vessel

After changing to the working frequency, each skipper should initially call with his or her boat's name, but the use of call signs is not required. After that, transmissions from each craft need not be identified, nor will the procedure word "Over" normally be necessary at the end of each transmission. You must limit the subject matter of your conversations on the air to what is legally permissible—necessary communications relating to the "needs of the ship." As mentioned before, communications that are "superfluous" are strictly prohibited. Each transmission and the whole contact should be as brief as possible. No station has exclusive rights to any specific channel and all must share. No station has priority over another except in safety communications.

Remember that at the end of the transmission each station must be identified by its FCC call sign (and usually the boat's name is also spoken). It is not necessary to give the call sign or name of the vessel with which you have been speaking.

## Emergency Communications

It is a good idea to learn how to radio for help in an emergency before one happens, rather than when you are in the midst of one. You will use the same calling procedures if you are ever in a position to assist another vessel in an emergency.

There are different levels of emergencies and different levels of priority for communications relating to emergencies. The highest priority is a Distress situation—limited to situations in which a vessel is "threatened by grave and imminent danger and requests immediate assistance." Radio traffic connected with a Distress situation is identified by the word "mayday" (derived from the French word meaning "help me.") Note carefully the high level of emergency required—do not call mayday if you are out of fuel or your engine will not start, or in any similar non-life-threatening situations. You may be in trouble, but you are not in distress: Use your radio to call for assistance, but don't preface your transmission with "mayday."

There are many distress situations that require immediate assistance, and some involve multiple emergencies. For example, let's say

> ## "MAYDAY"
> ## "PAN-PAN"
> ## "SECURITE"

*Figure 4.9 There are three levels of priority for radio transmissions. Do not use the highest level—MAYDAY—unless the situation is truly one of "distress". Know what the priority indicators mean and use them correctly.*

that in weathering a storm your sailboat is dismasted and a crewmember seems to have suffered a fractured skull from the falling spar, which has also holed the vessel close to the waterline. After identifying your vessel and its position, you inform the Coast Guard of the extent of injuries to your crewmember and the fact that your boat is taking on more water than the bilge pump can handle. In putting its SAR (Search and Rescue) team in action, the Coast Guard must have all these details. It must know whether to send an evacuation helicopter with a medical team and a pump on board, as well as surface vessels. The Coast Guard will advise you on interim care for the injured person, ask you to give a "long count" on the radio so they can position you, and advise you on how to prepare for the helicopter evacuation.

**If You Are in Distress**

Assuming that you are truly in distress, press your mike button (do not forget that essential action; it is sometimes overlooked in a crisis!), and transmit your "Distress Call." FCC regulations prescribe the use of a "radiotelephone alarm signal" of two specific audio tones transmitted alternately for a quarter second each. (This is a very effective attention-getter, and it is regrettable that it is not more often used. Circuitry for its automatic generation is built into few VHF transceivers, but its lack of use by shore-based Coast Guard units is difficult to understand.) If available, it is to be used at the

beginning of each Distress Call. The elements of a Distress Call are:
" mayday (spoken three times). This is (the name of your vessel spoken three times and your call sign) [803.15]. " After a brief pause, transmit the "Distress Message"—"mayday," your craft's name, your position, the nature of your distress, the kind of assistance requested, and other useful information, such as a description of your boat, the number and conditions of persons on board. Your position may be stated in terms of latitude and longitude, or direction and distance from a known geographical position or object. Then say, "I will be listening on Channel __ (fill in Channel 16 or 218 kHz as applicable). This is (the name of your vessel and your call sign). OVER." Speak slowly and distinctly—you must be understood as well as heard!

It is most desirable that you have a "preprepared" Distress Call and Message close to your radio. Record the vessel's name and call sign, and a good description of the vessel—length in feet, hull color, color of trim, sail rig, or other identifying features (see Appendix B). Type this up in as large a print as possible and get it sealed in plastic; place one copy near the radio and another in a secure place. The skipper is usually the "radio operator," but he or she may be in or part of the emergency, and another person unskilled in radio operation would then have to do the calling for help. There must always be at least two persons among those on board who know how to put the radio on the air.

Listen carefully for a reply—you are almost certainly going to get one, and probably too many! If possible, establish contact with the Coast Guard or another authority, but do not neglect the possibility of much faster response from another vessel that is closer. If you do not hear a reply, transmit again. If no reply is heard after several attempts on Channel 16, consider using another channel if you know one that is in local use. Don't give up; keep calling!

### If You Hear a Distress Call

If you are maintaining your watch on Channel 16 and you hear a Mayday call; *do not immediately respond.* Listen carefully for the Coast Guard or other authorities or a closer vessel to answer. Note the time of the emergency call and start taking notes of what you hear about the situation (or start your small tape recorder if you are using one for keeping a rough log for your vessel, an excellent procedure).

If after an interval of 30 to 60 seconds you hear no reply to the distressed vessel, or you hear it call a second time without an answer, you should respond using the following procedure: "Mayday (name or call sign of vessel in distress, spoken three times). This is (name of your vessel, spoken three times, your call sign), received mayday. OVER." You must then state your intentions by, for example, transmitting information on your position, the speed at which you are proceeding toward the distressed vessel, and your estimated time of arrival. Be sure, however, that such transmission will not interfere with messages of other stations responding to the situation. If you are not in a position to render assistance, and it appears that no one else has acknowledged the distress call, you must relay the information to the Coast Guard or other authorities. First, activate the radiotelephone alarm signal. Then make the following transmission: "Mayday relay (spoken three times). This is (your vessel's name spoken three times, your call sign, )." Follow this with the other vessel's distress message as you have received it. Then transmit, "I will be listening on Channel ___"(include channel and frequency, if possible), followed by your boat's name and call sign, and "OVER." Remember to speak slowly and distinctly.

## Radio Silence

Control of the distress traffic may be by the vessel in distress, but is more likely to be exercised by a Coast Guard unit. The controlling station will usually cut off normal use of Channel 16 by transmitting to "all stations," or any specific station, "seelonce mayday." If necessary, any other station can transmit seelonce distress, followed by its name and/or call sign. If you hear either of these transmissions, you must maintain radio silence on Channel 16. Make no transmissions on this frequency, but you may use other channels. The end of radio silence is announced by the station that imposed it with a message: "Hello all stations (spoken three times). This is (identification of the transmitting station). (Time.) (The name and call sign of the vessel that was in distress) seelonce feenee."

The reason for these seemingly odd phrases is that they must be recognizable to all persons regardless of their native language, and so they are internationally standardized.

### Distress Calls Using Digital Selective Calling

VHF sets are available that will automatically transmit a mayday call using Channel 70 rather than 16. Some models can be interfaced with your Loran receiver and include your position digitally encoded in the call. This feature will be of greater value after more vessels, and especially Coast Guard stations, have DSC equipment to receive such calls. At this time (1990), the automated DSC feature should be considered only a supplement to a normal distress call on Channel 16, not a replacement for it.

### Urgent Emergencies Other than Distress

A vessel may not be truly in distress as defined by the international radio regulations, but it may need to transmit an "Urgent" message, which is defined as one concerning the safety of a vessel or of some person on board or a potential problem that might lead to distress. Urgent messages may be a report of a person overboard (but only when help is required), or news of no steering or power in a shipping lane. Such transmissions are initiated with the Urgency signal, "PAN-PAN" (pronounced "pahn-pahn") spoken three times. This is followed by "All stations (or the name of a particular vessel). We (a statement of the nature of your emergency)." Then state the type of assistance you need and give other useful information, such as your position, a description of your vessel, or the number of people on board. End with your boat's name, your call sign, and "OVER."

Here is a typical example of the use of an Urgent message: While running off the coast on a weekend trip in your single-screw powerboat, you hit a submerged log so damaging your propeller that you are unable to continue without causing severe harm to your transmission system. No one aboard is injured and the boat is in no danger of sinking. However, night is coming on, the weather, according to NOAA weather radio, is deteriorating, and the seas are building. A "PAN-PAN" call identifying your vessel, giving its position, and the nature of your problem will alert vessels in your vicinity to your need and alert the Coast Guard to give priority to your emergency.

### Safety Call

The Safety Call, preceded by the word securite (say-curitay) spoken three times, is most often used by the Coast Guard to alert boat operators that the Coast Guard is preparing a safety message to be transmitted on another channel (usually 22A). The transmission may concern the loss of a navigation aid, an important meteorological message, a derelict afloat, or an overdue boat.

You may transmit a Safety Call as well. For instance, while heading out to sea from a major shipping channel, you spot a container awash near the entrance buoy. Obviously lost from a container ship, it is a menace to navigation, but you have no Coast Guard Safety Call on either Channel 16 or 22A. You call first on Channel 16 saying "SECURITE, SECURITE, SECURITE ALL STATIONS." Give your boat's name and call sign and say "Listen Channel 06 for a message." Then give your call sign and say "OUT." When you have switched to Channel 06, repeat "SECURITE, SECURITE, SECURITE ALL STATIONS" and again give your boat name and call sign. Then give the message, "There is a very large shipping container awash in the channel near buoy R2 at the entrance to Government Harbor." Sign off with your call sign and "OUT." You should also alert the Coast Guard by calling Channel 16 and switching to Channel 22A so that they can arrange to continue with further Safety Calls if needed and remove the obstacle.

## Bridge-to-Bridge Communications

The capability for direct voice communications between the conning officers of two ships approaching one another has added immensely

to the safety of navigation. Channel 13—the Bridge-to-Bridge channel—comes in handy for small boats when they transit a winding
channel with blind turns that is used by ships and tugs with barges.
In such cases, it is very helpful to have a dual-watch receiver so that
you can guard both Channels 16 and 13 essentially simultaneously.
Channel 13 is also very useful when you are approaching a dredge
working in a channel and are doubtful about when and on which
side it is safe to pass.

For such Bridge-to-Bridge communications, call directly on
Channel 13, using the name of the other vessel or dredge, if you know
it. Otherwise state a description of the unit you are calling, such as
"Tug pushing barges near Jamestown Bridge," or "Dredge working in
channel near day beacon 23." It is also permissible to state your position, such as when approaching a blind turn or about to enter a particularly narrow section of channel, and ask, "Any concerned traffic
respond on 13." Use 1-watt power only; and identify yourself with
your craft's name only—do not add your call sign. Keep your transmissions very brief. Don't neglect your watch on Channel 16.

Channel 13 is also used by highway and railroad drawbridge tenders; it is far superior to exchanging whistle signals. You can be
advised that the bridge will open immediately, or that there will be a
delay, and the reason therefor. The drawbridge operator may be monitoring Channel 16, and switching to 13 for traffic relating to the
opening. In some areas, however, drawbridge tenders guard Channel
13 only, so the initial call must be made on that frequency. Call the
bridge by name or location (the bridge station has call letters, but you
probably will not know them), and request that the bridge be opened.
Give your position and/or direction of travel. Use low power and
identify yourself with your vessel's name only. You must stay on
Channel 13 until you are safely through the opening in case the
bridge has to close suddenly or some other emergency arises.

## Communications with Private Coast Stations

Many marinas, yacht and boat clubs, towing services, and others are
licensed by the FCC to operate private coast stations. Coast stations
serving rivers, bays, and inland lakes (except the Great Lakes) must

maintain a watch on Channel 16 when they are open for business. They can, however, be excused from this requirement if a government station keeps such a watch that covers at least 95 percent of the coast station's normal service area.

Most other private coast stations also maintain a watch on Channel 16, but there are some that only monitor on a working channel. Facility listings and advertisements in cruising guides will usually note the channel that is monitored.

## Marine Operator Communications

VHF public coast (Marine Operator) stations normally monitor both Channel 16 and their working channel(s). Contact a local marine radio dealer for information on the channels of the Marine Operator stations in your boating area.

If you wish to make a land telephone connection, call the operator on the working channel—do not clutter up 16 with unnecessary transmissions. If that working channel is in use, you will hear a conversation. Use a different working channel, or if there is none, wait and try again later. Often you can be placed on a waiting list and be called back by the operator. The station will normally be identified by the geographic location and the words "Marine Operator." The operator will need to know your boat's name and call sign, and may need to know your general location, since some coast stations have more than one location for their receiving and transmitting antennas. Besides giving information about the number or person being called, you must arrange for payment for the service; this is best done by prior registration. Do not give credit card numbers over the radio. Call collect if necessary. Many public coast stations are operated by organizations other than the local telephone company, and these have their own billing and collection arrangements. (There is normally no additional charge beyond the established "linkage charge" for local calls, but, of course, normal long distance charges apply if the call must go farther.) In some areas you may be within range of two or more Marine Operators; if so, select the one for which there will be minimum landline charges.

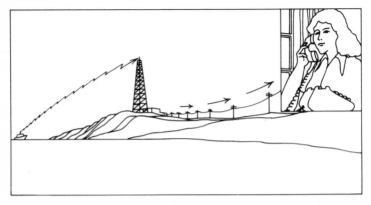

*Figure 4.10 When you are on your boat, you can use your VHF radio to make calls to telephones anywhere on land, and calls can be made to you. This is done through a "Marine Operator"; there are charges for this service, as well as any applicable long-distance charges.*

If a person at a shore telephone wishes to call you on your boat, he or she must call the appropriate Marine Operator. (Dial "0" and ask for the Boston Marine Operator, etc.) The Marine Operator will call your vessel on Channel 16 because that is where you are supposed to be listening. You will be told to reply to a specified Marine Operator. It is not necessary, and is undesirable, for you to acknowledge the call on 16. If you have made prior arrangements to be listening on the shore station's working channel in addition to Channel 16, the Marine Operator must call you there.

The FCC requirement for station identification every fifteen minutes is waived for communications through a public coast station, but you still must give your call sign at the end of the contact with the Marine Operator.

## Other VHF Radio Operations

Besides the activities discussed above, there are other types of communication with which you must be familiar. Of these, test transmissions and requests for signal reports are the most important.

## On-the-Air Tests

No station is permitted to cause harmful interference to the operation of other stations. You must not interfere with transmissions in progress. Test transmissions, as distinguished from requests for a signal report, may be necessary to determine proper antenna operation or adequate modulation. The FCC regulations require that you first transmit your station identification, followed by the word "Test" on the channel that is to be used. You must then delay briefly to give another station time to transmit the word "Wait" if it objects to your test transmissions. If you hear this response, you must wait for at least thirty seconds before repeating your initial call. When you hear no objections, you can continue with your test transmissions using number counts or word phrases that do not conflict with normal operating signals. Test transmissions must not continue for longer than 10 seconds and may not be repeated on Channel 16 for at least five minutes or on any other channel for at least one minute .

## Requests for Signal Reports

Modern VHF radio transceivers are very reliable items of electronic equipment—most of the calls for "Radio check" heard so frequently on the air are completely unnecessary. If, however, there is a real need to obtain a report on your transmission, there are prescribed procedures *and* limitations. First, general calls—calls not to a specific station—are strictly prohibited. The all-too-frequent call heard on Channel 16, "Anyone for a radio check," is a clear violation and subjects the operator to citation by the FCC. It is also in violation because the regulations prescribe that tests be made on a single-frequency working channel. Any report given in reply on 16 is a separate violation as an unauthorized use of that channel.

To get a report of your signal legally, use Channel 16 normally for initial contact with another station without going into why you are calling; do not call a Coast Guard station. Shift to a working channel in the usual manner, and then make your request for a signal report. An even better idea would be to listen on a working channel for two stations to conclude a conversation, and then quickly call one of them before it shifts back to 16.

The response to a request for a radio check should be clear and without the use of slang or CB lingo. If you hear a station well, say so: "I hear you loud and clear." (Do not use the word "read," for you are hearing something, not reading it from paper or a display screen.) Do not use "Five by five"; that is slang from military communications and not clearly meaningful to everyone. If you do not hear the other station well, say so directly: "I hear you weak but readable," or "You are loud but distorted," or "I am having difficulty in understanding you," or whatever words give a clear, unambiguous report on the other station's transmissions. Give the other operator the type of report that you would like to have on your signals.

Contacts with the Coast Guard for tests on Channel 16 may be made only by representatives of the FCC during inspections (applicable to compulsory installations), or when licensed technicians are making a new installation, or if requested by the Coast Guard. Such tests must be identified as "FCC" or "technical" as appropriate.

**Operation of Hand-Held Sets**

As noted before, a hand-held VHF transceiver can be used as the basic radio on a boat under the station license for the vessel. Such a set also may be operated as an "associated ship unit" off the vessel but in the vicinity, such as on a dinghy. As such, it can only be used on Channel 16 and commercial or noncommercial intership working channels as determined by the status of the parent vessel. Power must be limited to one watt. Except for safety purposes, you can only use it for communications with the parent craft, or with other similar units associated with the same parent craft. The call sign is that of the parent vessel followed by an appropriate unit designator (such as "Mobile" or "Unit 1"). *A hand-held set may never be operated on shore, not even to call the parent vessel.*

Do not forget to recharge the battery of your hand-held set after you have used it so that it will be ready for the next use. It is desirable, however, to run the battery down all the way every month or two, and then immediately to recharge it fully. This will prevent the Ni-Cad cells from developing a "memory," which would limit their capacity. If a memory condition should develop—indicated by significantly shortened battery life—you may have to "deep discharge" and recharge several times to restore full capacity. Use only a charger designed for your radio—polarities and voltages vary. Do not leave the batteries on charge longer than the time period stated in the manual for the set, typically twelve to fifteen hours.

### Continuous Weather Broadcasts

The National Weather Service (NWS) operates many VHF-FM radio stations around the country that transmit continuous weather reports and forecasts on frequencies that can be received by marine VHF transceivers. These channels are generally designated as "WX-1," "WX-2." Some sets advertise "ten weather channels," but only seven are in use in the United States, and only three by more than 90 percent of the stations. Marine weather information for Canadian waters is broadcast on different frequencies, but is still receivable on VHF marine sets.

The three primary weather channels are assigned geographically to minimize interference. Coverage is essentially complete for all coastal waters and many inland areas. The range of any given NWS transmitter is normally about 40 miles, but many have tall antennas and reach farther. In some boating areas, more than one station can be heard. Some broadcasts are "paired"—that is, the same taped message is transmitted from two geographic locations to achieve broader coverage.

### Radio Logs

Radio stations on voluntarily equipped (recreational) craft are not required to maintain a routine radio station log. They should, however, record information on any distress traffic they engaged in or heard. A record of the name and license number of any technician who works on the set is also desirable.

Compulsorily equipped vessels must maintain radio station logs, with the content varying with the type of vessel. Required station documents for these vessels may include a copy of the FCC Rules and Regulations, operator licenses, station lists, and various safety certificates; again, these requirements will vary with the type of vessel.

**Secrecy Provisions**

The basic Communications Act, the authority for all radio regulations, contains specific provisions for ensuring the security of communications. It is expressly forbidden to divulge the contents of any communications you hear on the radio to anyone other than the addressee, his or her agent or attorney, or persons involved in the handling of such communications unless authorized to do so by the sender. Not only is a person receiving or intercepting communications prohibited from improperly divulging their contents, but that person is also prohibited from using such information for his or her own benefit or that of others.

Exceptions are made for communications relating to distress situations and for broadcasts intended for the use of the general public. The contents of amateur radio communications are also not protected by the secrecy restrictions.

# CHAPTER FIVE

# FCC VIOLATIONS AND PENALTIES

T he use of radio transmitters, and some other electronic equipment, is governed by laws—Acts of Congress—and by implementing regulations—the FCC Rules and Regulations. To put "teeth" into the enforcement of these restrictions, there is a series of penalties for violations. If you know the regulations relating to your radio operation, and are careful to follow them, you should never be concerned with this chapter.

If an FCC monitoring station or field inspector detects you in a violation of a law or regulation, you may be sent either a warning or a citation; the form that you receive will clearly indicate which it is. If you receive a warning, you should carefully review the circumstances of the incident and refresh your memory of the applicable regulations. You are not required to make any official reply, but you can correspond with the issuing FCC office if you are not certain what the violation was.

*If you receive a citation, you must reply within the time period stated;* this is normally 10 days [80.149]. To fail to reply within the required time is a further violation, with penalties beyond those for the initial offense. If you cannot make a complete reply at that time, make an interim acknowledgment of receipt of the citation, give what information you can, and state when you will be able to submit more complete data. If receipt of the citation has been delayed—as might occur when you are off cruising in an area distant from your home address—reply immediately upon receipt and explain the delay.

The response to the FCC should be addressed to the office that issued the citation. Each communication must be complete in itself and not shortened by references to prior correspondence or answers to other notices. Each reply must be submitted in duplicate. The answer to a citation must contain a full explanation of the incident involved and the steps taken to prevent a continuation or recurrence. If the notice relates to a lack of attention to, or improper operation of, the station, or to log or watchkeeping discrepancies, the answer must give the name and license number of the licensed operator on duty. (This latter requirement is not applicable if the circumstances did not require a licensed operator.)

## Penalties

Violation of radio laws and regulations can result in administrative actions or criminal charges. Penalties can include fines or imprisonment, or both.

### Administrative Forfeitures

The lowest level of penalty that may be given to you for violation of an FCC regulation is termed an administrative forfeiture. This is a form of civil fine that can be assessed against you without a court appearance. Forfeitures are used for certain violations of which the ones most likely to concern licensees of stations on boats are:

- Failure to identify the station at the times and in the manner prescribed by the regulations.
- Transmission of any unauthorized communications on a distress or calling frequency.
- Operation of a station without a valid permit or a license of the proper grade.
- Interference with a distress call or distress communications.
- Transmission of any false call contrary to the regulations.
- Failure to respond to an official communication from the FCC.

# CHAPTER SIX

# MF/HF Single-Sideband Radio

S ingle-sideband radio provides a voice for mariners venturing beyond the 20-mile ship-to-ship and ship-to-shore range of VHF radio. While all vessels must carry VHF before they install SSB, no prudent skipper would go offshore without SSB, knowing that its range is practically limitless, depending upon the time of day and atmospheric conditions. Marine SSB transceivers operate within the medium-frequency and high-frequency portions of the radio spectrum—2 to 22 MHz—on seven bands that can provide a range from 150 miles to worldwide.

## Modulation Methods

The term "single sideband" refers to the type of modulation that is used to carry the voice information on the radio circuit. The VHF band uses frequency modulation—the radio frequency is varied by an audio rate; the signals are very clear and of excellent quality. This form of modulation, however, takes up considerable space in the radio spectrum, space that is available in VHF bands, but not in the lower MF and HF bands. The modulation that must be used on those frequencies is amplitude modulation, in which the strength of the signal is varied by the voice wave form. For many decades of radio transmitting, the radiated signal consisted of a carrier wave with half of the signal power and two sidebands, each with a quarter of the signal power. The sidebands were both above and below the carrier wave and transmitted the same information, while the carrier was needed but provided no information. This is double-sideband (DSB) modulation. With advanced technology, equipment design and components improved to the point where it was no longer necessary to radiate the carrier wave and both sidebands—since the carrier wave robbed power and one sideband was merely a mirror image of the other. All that is required now is a single sideband, hence the name for this modulation technique.

The suppression of the carrier has a further advantage in lessening the interference between two signals on the same frequency or close to each other. Single-sideband signals take up less than half the space in the radio spectrum that was needed by the older, double-sideband AM signals. This allows many more channels to be used and more communications to be carried on at the same time.

There are several variations of single-sideband modulation, determined by the extent to which the carrier and unwanted sideband are suppressed. Fully suppressed signals, designated as J3E by the FCC, are normally used. A reduced "pilot" carrier signal is required for some communications; this mode is designated as R3E. For contacts with some foreign stations that have not converted from the old double-sideband mode of operation, there is a full-carrier single-sideband mode, H3E; this is sometimes called "AM Equivalent" or "Compatible AM."

The significance of SSB for you is that, with J3E signals, the full power of your transmitter is used in transmitting your voice, giving you greater range and clearer communications.

**Frequency Bands**

A number of small "slices" of the overall radio spectrum in the MF and HF regions are allocated for maritime SSB voice communications. (Different segments are allocated for radiotelegraphy—Morse code—facsimile, and radioprinter communications.) Distances that can be reached vary with the frequency used, the time of day, the season, and even the status of the 11-year sunspot cycle. The information given below for each band must be used only as a general guide; conditions are too variable for exact statements.

• 2 MHz—Usable for shorter distances of up to about 150 miles in the daytime and roughly twice that distance at night. Note, however, that if you are within VHF range of the other station you must use VHF.

• 4 MHz—Used for short to medium distances of up to 250 miles during the day, with ranges of 150 to 1,500 miles at night.

• 6 MHz—Used for medium distances, up to 250 miles in daytime, extending to 2,000 miles at night. This band is used more on the Mississippi River and connecting waters than elsewhere.

• 8 MHz—Usable for medium distances, 250-1,500 miles during the day, and longer distances of 400-3,000 miles at night.

There are also marine SSB allocations at 12, 16, and 22 MHz—all long-distance bands with ranges of thousands of miles. These frequencies are particularly susceptible to the effects of time of day, season, and sunspot conditions.

**Specific Channels**

Channel number designations are used in the SSB service, but not to the extent that they are in VHF communications; direct statement of the frequency is often used. The FCC has established channel numbers for most, but not all, duplex frequency pairs. These consist of groups of three or four digits; the first one or two digits indicate the frequency band—such as 4 MHz or 12 MHz—and the latter two digits are assigned arbitrarily.

Specific frequencies, or frequency pairs, are assigned for distress, calling and reply, safety, intership, and ship-to-coast radiotelephone communications, and for contacts with the Coast Guard.

The most important SSB frequency is 2182 kHz, an international distress and calling/answering channel equivalent to Channel 16 on the VHF band. (In the 2 MHz band, frequencies are usually stated in kiloHertz—1 MHz = 1,000 kHz.) Various other 2 MHz band frequencies are allocated for intership safety and other communications, some usable in all geographic areas and others restricted to specific areas, such as the Great Lakes and the Gulf of Mexico. Use of two of the geographically restricted frequencies, 2738.0 and 2830.0 kHz, is permitted outside their areas if the distance is less than 200 miles and one of the stations is within the specified area. Aircraft can use these two frequencies to communicate with ship stations subject to limitations of necessity—if there is no interference to intership contacts, and if the power does not exceed 25 watts. The frequency 2670 kHz is used for communications with the Coast Guard.

The FCC has also designated the frequency 8364 kHz for use by vessels in distress—the HF equivalent of 2182 kHz. This is normally used for single-sideband transmissions, but in distress situations any form of modulation and as much power as is obtainable can be used.

The following simplex frequencies also may be used by coast and ship stations for distress and safety communications: 4125.0, 6215.5, 8257.0, 12,392.0, and 16,522.0. (On 1 July 1991, the frequency 8257.0 will be replaced with 8291.0 for distress and safety communications.) Aircraft may use 4125.0 for traffic to ships. Note that these are not calling frequencies with mandatory listening watches. A separate set of frequencies is provided for distress and safety calling, using digital selective calling (DSC) techniques.

The Coast Guard operates a Contact and Long-Range Liaison (CALL) service using one frequency pair in each of the 4, 6, 8, 12, and 16 MHz bands.

For operational and business communications between ship and coast stations and between ship stations, there are three or more simplex frequencies assigned in each band. All these frequencies are shared by all stations, except that a private coast station will not normally be assigned to use more than one frequency in any band. There are minor geographic restrictions and special provisions for the CALL service.

Ship-to-shore communications on the lower frequencies are divided into two services—Regional and High Seas. The Regional Service provides wider coverage than the Local/Harbor Service of VHF stations. It operates primarily on the 2 MHz band, but there is a limited number of HF channels assigned for the Great Lakes and the Mississippi River System. Both single-frequency simplex channels and two-frequency duplex channels are used. Stations may be from one to seven channels.

The High Seas Service uses channels in the 4 MHz and higher frequency bands for even wider coverage. (Some stations operate in the Regional and/or Local Services in addition to the High Seas Service.) All channels are dual frequency for duplex operation, and channel designators are commonly used instead of specific frequencies. Call and reply channels for ships and shore stations are also established, with one frequency-pair in each of the 8, 12, 16, and 22 MHz bands; these are not working frequencies.

Specific sub-bands are set up for radioprinter transmissions between ship and private coast stations using authorized frequencies within these bands.

Details of these rather complex channel assignments will be found with each SSB set purchased. Because the assignments change from time to time, such information should be verified and updated at intervals.

## Licenses for SSB Communications

As with all radio transmitters, equipment used on vessels for single-sideband communications must have an FCC station license. A license for VHF use is not sufficient, although a VHF radio must be on board before an SSB is purchased. Specific authorization is required for operation on frequencies of 1,600 to 4,000 kHz and 4,000 to 23,000 kHz, but these are included on the same form. A request for SSB frequencies can be made at the time of application for the basic VHF station license; if SSB operation is likely to be desired at any time in the future, the appropriate boxes should be checked on Form 506 before it is submitted to the FCC.

If SSB operation was not requested at the time of the original application, you must apply for a modified station license using FCC Form 506, with all boxes checked for the frequencies desired. The fee for the modification of the license is $35, and FCC Form 155 must be included (as discussed in Chapter 3); the Fee Type Code is "PAS."

## Operator Permits

An operator license is required for SSB operation on all waters. For voluntarily equipped (recreational) craft, a Restricted Radiotelephone Operator Permit is sufficient. This assumes that the equipment has been installed and tuned by a person holding the proper grade of commercial radio operator license, and that operation of the SSB set involves only turning a knob or pushing a button or buttons to change frequency.

For compulsorily equipped craft, such as those carrying more than six passengers for hire, a Marine Radio Operator Permit is required.

# CHAPTER SEVEN

# SINGLE-SIDEBAND EQUIPMENT AND OPERATION

For single-sideband communications you need a transceiver and antenna, as you do with VHF. But SSB equipment is more complex, and somewhat larger and more expensive than its equivalent on VHF. The greater bulk is not a major problem, but it will increase the minimum size of craft on which they can be installed. The antenna is more of a problem than the transceiver.

## Transceiver Selection

The factors that influence the selection of an SSB set create a wider choice than for a VHF transceiver. The quality of the sets is assured because of FCC Type Acceptance. Be sure that you don't make a commitment for equipment marked "Type Acceptance pending." There is a range of output power levels, channel capacities, and special features from which to choose.

### Output Power

The FCC regulations set maximum power limits for SSB transmitters according to the waters in which the vessel operates and the frequencies used. For all Great Lakes and inland waters, the maximum limit is 150 watts. For open waters, on frequencies between 2,000 and 4,000 kHz, the limit is also 150 watts, except on the distress frequency of 2182 kHz, where power up to 400 watts may be used. For open waters and frequencies of 4,000 to 27,500 kHz, the maximum power is 1,500 watts.

Many sets are manufactured with 150 watts of output power, and this level should meet the needs of all mariners on all waters and

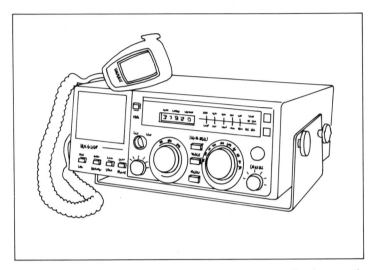

*Figure 7.1 Transceivers for SSB communications are somewhat larger and more expensive than VHF sets. The antennas are larger and the installations more complex, but these radios are required if you must communicate beyond VHF range.*

frequencies. Some models are available with only 100 watts; this should be sufficient for most craft, although power is more important on SSB frequencies than on VHF channels.

### Frequency Bands and Numbers of Channels

The range of a single-sideband radiotelephone can extend from several hundred to many thousands of miles, with the higher frequencies covering the greatest distances. Among smaller vessels, only world-cruising yachts need the greater coverage. Channels in the lower four or five frequency bands will be adequate to reach a stateside Marine Operator from Caribbean or Canadian waters. Thus a set with an upper limit of the 12-MHz band is sufficient for all normal uses, and the greater expense for sets that will reach up to 22 MHz channels can be avoided. An upper limit of 8 MHz will satisfy the needs of most skippers, and may be even less costly. All sets cover the 2 MHz channel.

Although the receivers and transmitters of most SSB radios can be tuned to all channels within their frequency range, each set has a limited number of channels that can be pretuned for quick access and use. Some models will have provision for eight to 12 preset channels—sufficient for all ordinary applications. Modern digital technology, however, has made possible transceivers that can be programmed for hundreds of channels, not that there is any real need for so many. Channels may be selected by a rotary knob or key pad. Many sets are sold with a number of preprogrammed channels, plus the ability to program additional frequencies. Programmed channels are tuned in easily and quickly; nonprogrammed frequencies are brought up by key pad entries. On some models, an LCD frequency display can also show a brief name for each programmed channel; this will greatly simplify selection of the frequency you want.

**Special Features**

To reduce the bulk of the transceiver, which must be mounted within easy reach of the skipper, some sets are now being manufactured in two units. One or more small control heads are connected by cable to the main transceiver so that it can be mounted out of sight in any convenient location. In a few models the connector is a "high-tech," fiber-optic cable not much larger than the lead in an ordinary wooden pencil.

Many SSB transceivers now feature "memory channels" that permit even faster and easier selection of frequently used channels. Scanning of these channels is also possible.

A separate direct selector for the distress frequency, 2182 kHz, is very desirable. Also desirable is internal circuitry for generating the radiotelephone alarm signal; two high-pitched audio tones transmitted alternately are a most effective attention-getter. This may be a standard feature or an option that can be ordered separately.

Another desirable feature is a controllable audio squelch, standard on VHF sets, but not included on all SSB transceivers.

More and more transceivers are being designed to have a serial output (RS–232) terminal for connection with a radio modem. This permits the receipt of facsimile ("fax") signals, or the receipt and transmittal of digital data.

Marine SSB transceivers may legally be used on ham radio bands by a licensed amateur, but not vice versa (see Chapter 9). A possible complication, however, is that hams use the lower-sideband mode on some frequencies, but all marine transmissions are standardized on the upper sideband. A few marine SSB sets may have a front-panel control for sideband selection, but most will require an internal modification if this capability is needed. Don't forget that ham operation, while very useful, requires separate licenses for both the station and the operator.

If the receiver portion of your SSB set can be tuned to any frequency, you can use it to listen to shortwave broadcasts and other interesting signals. The receiver should be able to tune to frequencies well below the marine SSB bands, as low as 500 kHz.

# Antenna Systems for SSB Sets

The antenna requirements for a single-sideband installation are much more complex and stringent than for VHF equipment. Note carefully the use of the term "system." The system consists of the antenna and a ground connection, with an antenna tuner to match these components to the transceiver. Each plays a vital part, and each must be operating properly for optimum communications. Nothing will so limit the performance of an SSB set as an inadequate antenna system.

### The Antenna and the Tuner

Antennas for single-sideband installations on powerboats consist of a metallic radiating element within an outer fiberglass sheath. Externally, these look like the antennas typically used for marine VHF stations, except that they are considerably longer. They are generally the size of 9-dB VHF antennas, roughly 23 feet in length. The SSB antenna is larger because of the lower frequencies used, but even so it is far shorter than the ideal, particularly on the lower frequency bands. Artificial electronic means must be employed to make the antenna appear to the transceiver to be longer than it actually is—this is where a tuner becomes a part of the system.

On sailboats a portion of a backstay is normally used as an antenna by installing insulators near the top and bottom. Used with a proper tuner, such an antenna can be more effective than the whip

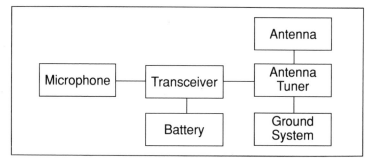

*Figure 7.2  A proper antenna and ground connection are essential for successful SSB operation; without them your communications range will be severely limited. Installation of your set is a job for a qualified and experienced technician.*

used on a powerboat. Multimasted craft can sometimes install an antenna between two masts if the spacing is great enough to provide adequate antenna length.

An antenna tuner consists of a metal box housing several inductances (coils) and capacitors, with knobs to control their values and switches to interconnect them in different circuit arrangements. In remotely or automatically controlled tuners, the switches are replaced by relays. Some SSB transceivers have a built-in antenna tuner or its equivalent, but many rely on an external unit. (Often the antenna tuner is priced as an "option," but it is definitely a necessity!) Ideally the tuner will be located at or near the base of the antenna; this is the advantage of having a separate unit. The transceiver and tuner are interconnected by a coax cable, such as RG-8/U, and a control cable for remotely operated units. For the greatest ease of operation, the tuner should adjust automatically.

**The Ground System**

The radio frequency (RF) ground system is a vital part of a single-sideband installation. (Connecting the negative power lead to the boat's electrical system "grounds" the equipment for DC, but is not adequate for radio frequencies.) An SSB antenna operates as half of a dipole radiator—you can think of it as the antenna projecting upward and a mirror image projecting downward. It is the ground system that provides the lower half; without it the system operates poorly, if at all.

The essence of an RF ground for SSB sets is adequate area—the more the better. The ground can be a copper plate on the outside of the hull, which is what was used in the old days. But now, with the near-universal use of fiberglass, the trend is to include an area of copper screening within the layers of the hull as the craft is constructed. Of course, if the hull is a metal, such as aluminum, the problem is solved. It is not necessary that the "ground plate" be in contact with the water; the copper screen within a fiberglass hull has sufficient capacitive coupling at radio frequencies.

## Selecting SSB Equipment

In selecting a specific SSB transceiver and antenna, you will not be faced with as many brands and models as for VHF equipment, but there are nevertheless many manufacturers and still more models. Choose a set that is adequate for your needs, but don't go for capabilities and features that aren't really necessary for you and that add to the cost. If possible, choose a manufacturer who has a dealer located conveniently to where you keep your boat—you will need help with the installation and may need service later, and paid service time for technicians usually starts the minute they leave their shop.

If you are not going blue-water cruising, you don't need the ability to operate on the 16- and 22-MHz bands or, probably, on the 12-MHz band. There is nothing wrong with having such capabilities, but they often add to the cost of the set and antenna tuner. Memory channels are useful, but you are not going to be changing channels as often as you do on VHF. Scanning is also useful, but rarely needed. Generation of the radiotelephone alarm signal is very desirable, but not absolutely necessary if it is not available on a set that is otherwise satisfactory for your needs. You won't notice much difference between output power levels of 100 and 150 watts, but don't go lower. To summarize: Get a good quality set with the necessary features, but don't buy beyond your real needs.

There will be little choice in the size of the antenna. As mentioned earlier, the antenna will typically be a fiberglass whip of about 23 feet in length. The base fitting will come as a part of the antenna, but you also will need an upper support bracket. Get the best!

Again, as with VHF sets, try to find someone with an SSB radio of the general type you are looking for and ask that person about his or her satisfaction with the equipment and dealer service (service satisfaction is more important here than with VHF sets).

## Installation

Proper installation is critical to the successful operation of an SSB radiotelephone. If you are handy with tools, you will not find it difficult to install the set and connect it to a source of electrical power. The "radio" part of the installation, however, must be done by an individual who is properly licensed, and should be done by someone who is experienced in this task. Each installation is unique when it comes to getting the optimum performance from the transceiver and its antenna system. A person who has faced these problems before, and solved them, will get the better results, and in less time.

The SSB transceiver can be located anywhere on the boat where it can conveniently be operated and is protected from rain and spray. It is less likely than with VHF that you will be operating an SSB set while simultaneously steering your craft. SSB radios are often installed below decks in the main cabin or at the navigation station. If you buy a two-piece set, you can put the control unit at a convenient location, with the bulkier main unit out of sight almost anyplace. The distance from the transceiver output to the antenna, or antenna tuner to antenna, should be as short as is practicable.

The DC power drain of an SSB transceiver is greater than that of a VHF set; follow the manufacturer's recommendations on the gauge of the wire supplying power to the set.

Because of its size, the base of an SSB antenna on a powerboat must be located where it is also possible to mount an upper support bracket; this may limit your choice of a site. The physical force can be considerable when a large antenna whips about as the boat rolls and pitches in heavy seas. Choose firm, strong surfaces for both the base and the upper bracket.

The wire from the antenna tuner—internal or external—to the antenna may look like coax cable, but it is not. It is merely a single strand of wire, usually 12-gauge, with insulation for very high voltages—a typical wire is designated "GTO-15." Use a watertight fitting to bring the antenna lead through the side of the boat and into the interior; make sure you have a drip loop (see Fig. 4.6) and sufficient slack between the antenna and fitting to lower the antenna.

## Maintenance

About all you can do to maintain your SSB radio yourself is replace a blown fuse or circuit breaker—if a second fuse of the proper size blows immediately or the breaker trips, stop right there! Do not attempt to solve the problem by installing a higher-rated fuse; by doing so you could damage the set, or even cause a fire. If you hear no signals, but are receiving background noise, check that your antenna lead-in has not come loose. Beyond this, it will be necessary to call in a licensed and qualified technician. Be sure that you can clearly explain the difficulties being encountered before you call—you might be able to solve the problem from the technician's suggestions, and certainly you can eliminate a costly second trip for special tools or parts.

As with VHF antennas, a "weathered" appearance to the outer fiberglass shell of an SSB antenna can be corrected by the application of a light coat of resin or varnish. If the insulation of the antenna lead-in wire becomes cracked from exposure to sun and sea spray, the wire should be replaced. You can do the job, provided that you use the correct type of wire.

If you use your sailboat's backstay for an antenna, make sure that salt and dirt deposits from the atmosphere don't lessen the effectiveness of the insulators. Rain will normally wash away such deposits, but in a dry spell it may be necessary to wash them off yourself periodically.

# OPERATING YOUR SINGLE-SIDEBAND RADIO

First, remember that if you are within VHF range of the other station, then the VHF band must be used. Next, if you are going to use SSB communications, you must decide what band to use. The frequency-distance relationships given in the preceding chapter are a useful starting point, but are not always exact. Unless you have experience to guide you, listen on channels of the most likely band for stations at the distance over which you wish to talk; this is especially useful for calls to Marine Operator stations. Then consult any available source for the specific frequencies within the selected band that are proper for the type of communications you desire to use.

### Mandatory Listening Watch

Voluntarily equipped vessels—recreational boats and craft carrying less than six passengers for hire—are not required to have their SSB radios turned on while afloat, nor are they required to maintain a watch on any specified frequency if the set is on. However, 2182 kHz is an international distress and calling/answering frequency, and if you are listening, you may be of help to some vessel requiring assistance or information; or you may hear someone trying to get in contact with you. Many SSB transceivers have an audio squelch control that allows you to silence the background noise while still listening on the frequency; there is not as much traffic on this channel as there is on VHF Channel 16.

A craft carrying more than six passengers for hire must keep a continuous watch on 2182 kHz when it is beyond the communication range of the nearest VHF coast station. (This is in addition to the Channel 16 watch that must be maintained whether or not within range of a coast station.) Additional equipment is not required, as these watches need not be maintained while the respective radios are being used for communications with another station. Larger, compulsorily equipped vessels also must maintain a watch on 2182 kHz, and some must do so with an automatic radiotelephone alarm receiver, as well as the watch on VHF Channel 16.

## General Operating Procedures

The general operating procedures on SSB frequencies are similar to those described in Chapter 4 for VHF Systems and will not be repeated here. For details about who may talk on your radio, station identification, procedure words, and so forth, refer to that chapter.

SSB transceivers and separate receivers have a front-panel control often called a "clarifier." This permits you to slightly adjust the receiver frequency to make the incoming voice more natural and easier to understand. Leave this control at its center or zero position unless it is needed.

### Intership Communications

When you have decided upon the frequency band and specific channel to be used, listen before you transmit. You must not cause interference to communications in progress, and SSB signals cover far wider areas than VHF, with a consequent greater potential for interference to others. For distances over which 2 MHz signals can be heard, 2182 kHz is a calling frequency on which many stations will be listening. On the 4 MHz band, the simplex frequency 4125.0 kHz is used internationally for calling, but no similarly designated channels exist for higher-frequency bands. On SSB radio, however, it is more likely that your initial contacts will be made directly on a prearranged working channel at a scheduled time.

Initial calls should be made in the same manner as on VHF; you will need to state the name of the called vessel two or three times, as SSB communications are rarely as noise-free and clear as those on VHF. The same rules apply as on VHF about the required time intervals before calls can be repeated, and the duration of any given call. If contact is made on a calling channel, reach agreement on a working frequency and shift immediately. Make sure that your conversation on the working channel is restricted to authorized topics; subject matter that is superfluous to necessary communications is prohibited. Be sure to give full identification of your station, including your call sign, when you close your conversation with the other station.

### Emergency Communications

When using SSB radio, emergency communications must be carried out even more carefully than on VHF, because the stations that you need to reach are probably at greater distances, and receiving

| You Transmit | You Receive |
|---|---|
| 4134.3 MHz | 4428.7MHz |
| 6200.0 MHz | 6506.4 MHz |
| 8241.5 MHz | 8765.4 MHz |
| 12342.4 MHz | 13113.2 MHz |

*Figure 7.3 The Coast Guard monitors certain SSB frequencies as part of its Contact and Long Range Liaison (CALL) system. These frequencies are also used for voice weather broadcasts and emergency communications, including essential navigation information and medical assistance.*

conditions may be less satisfactory.

The MF distress frequency is 2182 kHz. By international treaties, laws, and regulations, ships and shore stations will be maintaining a listening watch on this channel. Use this frequency first, but if you do not receive a reply after two or three calls, do not hesitate to shift to another channel, preferably one on which you hear activity, intership or ship-to-shore. In U.S. waters, the frequency 4125.0 kHz is also available for distress and safety communications. The Coast Guard monitors 2182 kHz, of course, but also has pairs of half-duplex frequencies on higher-frequency bands. (See Fig. 7.3 for a list of these frequencies.) Coast Guard units may have only one transmitter to use on all these frequencies, so you may not get an immediate response; allow at least one minute before deciding that you have not been heard.

The various levels of emergencies and priorities, distress calls and messages, and actions to be taken if you hear a distress call, or for an imposition of radio silence, are the same for SSB as for VHF (see Chapter 4). Do not use "mayday" unless you have a valid distress situation involving the safety of life or property that requires immediate assistance. Know the meaning of the other priority indicators—pan-pan and securite—and use them appropriately. Be sure to precede a distress call with the radiotelephone alarm signal if your transceiver is so equipped (and this is far more likely to be the case on SSB sets than on VHF sets).

## Communications with Coast Stations

In SSB communications, most contacts with private coast stations are those of commercial fishing and towing vessels talking with their home bases. Procedures are generally the same as for VHF communications, except that nearly all contacts are prearranged as to time and frequency. The FCC rules do not prohibit such communications, but there are far fewer private shore stations on these frequencies than on VHF, and the likelihood of needing such communications is much less.

SSB public coast stations are classified as "regional" and "high seas" (the VHF service is termed "local"). These descriptive terms are self-evident; the regional public coast stations are located along the coasts, Great Lakes, and the Mississippi River system and use frequencies in the 2 MHz band. The inland stations are also authorized channels from higher-frequency bands. The high-seas stations are fewer in number, cover wider expanses of the oceans, and use HF channels. (They also may operate on a 2 MHz channel for their immediate areas.) Each public coast station is assigned its own channels so as not to interfere with others. If you anticipate a need for SSB Marine Operator communications, contact a marine radio dealer in your boating area for current information on specific channels that you may need. On higher-frequency bands, there are "calling and reply" frequency pairs for use with coast stations, but no mandatory watches.

As with VHF, you must shift to an authorized working frequency to carry on your communications on SSB radio; but contacts will also be established directly on a working channel. Calls may originate from individuals on shore, and if this is a possibility in your case, you should ensure that such persons know the proper station to use and how to reach that station by telephone. AT&T High-Seas Operators may be reached by dialing 1-800-sea-call. Other High-Seas Operators have their own 800 numbers.

High-seas stations normally broadcast "traffic lists" hourly or at scheduled times, but these may be omitted if the station is busy with ongoing communications. These lists include the names (and call sign, if known) of all vessels for whom the shore station is holding calls.

Charges for ship-to-shore calls via AT&T stations are billed as person-to-person calls regardless of whether they are directed to an individual or only to a number. Charges are based on a per minute rate with a three-minute minimum. This is a flat rate without regard for the distance from the coast station to the called telephone anywhere in the United States, Canada, Mexico, Puerto Rico, and the U.S. Virgin Islands. Calls to overseas points may be made with charges comparable to those for calls from a telephone on shore. There is no charge for distress communications connected through to the Coast Guard. Vessels should preregister for billing purposes, or calls can be charged to the called party or a third number, such as the caller's home or office phone. Other high-seas and coastal stations have their own rate schedules.

Don't overlook the potential of using public coast stations in cases of emergencies. On SSB radio you can often reach a Marine Operator more easily and quickly than you can reach the Coast Guard. Marine Operators will accept a mayday call and patch you through to the appropriate U.S. Coast Guard unit or other search and rescue service. You can then set up continuing communications on a Coast Guard working frequency or other channel.

**Other SSB Radio Operations**

Due to equipment complexity and general operating conditions, test transmissions and requests for signal reports are more likely to be needed with SSB radios than with VHF sets. The same FCC regulations and operating procedures are generally applicable. A test transmission on 2182 kHz may not be repeated for five minutes. Use a working channel for tune-up and equipment checks. Calls may be made to coast or other ship stations for signal reports if necessary; 2182 kHz may be used, but a working channel is preferable. The same restrictions as for VHF apply to test calls to Coast Guard units.

**Weather and Marine Information Broadcasts**

There are no continuous weather information broadcasts on SSB, as there are on VHF, but public coast stations and Coast Guard communications stations broadcast weather reports and forecasts on

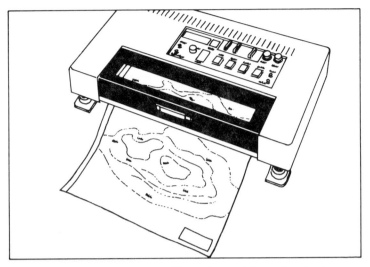

*Figure 7.4 Weather maps can provide much more information about coming conditions than voice broadcasts. They can be obtained using special receiver/printer combinations, or a modem and printer can be attached to your regular SSB transceiver and personal computer.*

a scheduled basis. Information on the schedules may be obtained from the commercial stations or Coast Guard district offices. The Coast Guard units also broadcast marine information regarding aids to navigation, hazards, and other safety items.

Radio facsimile broadcasts provide weather maps that can be received and printed out for study. You can use a complete facsimile receiver or a stand-alone printer that will decode signals received on a transceiver or separate receiver. With appropriate software, a personal computer and printer can also produce weather maps from these signals by processing them through a special modem unit.

**Violations and Penalties**

The FCC provisions for violations and penalties described in Chapter 5 also apply to SSB communications. The requirements for a radio station log are the same for SSB and for VHF radio operations.

# CHAPTER EIGHT

# CITIZENS BAND RADIO

Although not truly a marine service, Citizens Band Radio (CB) offers certain advantages to boaters. The equipment is small, inexpensive, and easy to install. However, CB is not a substitute for VHF marine radio as a safety service. Nor is it a substitute for SSB marine communications, as long-distance transmissions on CB channels are not reliable and are not legal for informal communication at distances greater than 250 km (155 miles).

## About Citizens Band

The primary purpose of CB radio is local communications. The normal range is roughly 5 miles, but this can be increased by antenna height and by using directional antennas at fixed stations.

CB communications take place on 40 channels near 29 MHz—lower in frequency than the marine VHF band—and are quite sensitive to the time of day, the season, and particularly the status of the sunspot cycle. These factors affect both the distance over which signals may be heard and the interference level. CB transmissions are ground-wave signals; sky-wave signals from great distances may sometimes be heard. Most CB radios use double-sideband (AM) modulation. Single-sideband is available but is considerably more expensive.

### FCC Regulations

Federal regulations for CB use state that communications may not be related to illegal activities and, as on all radio services, transmissions

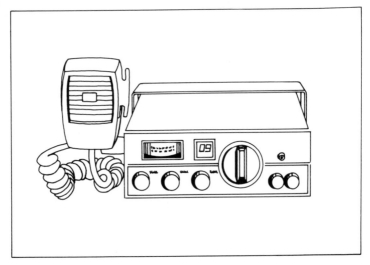

*Figure 8.1  A CB radio can be of considerable value on a boat, for it can be used for personal and social communications that are prohibited on marine VHF channels. Do not , however, consider such a set a substitute for a marine VHF radio for safety communications.*

may not contain profane, indecent, or obscene language. Beyond that there is little limitation. Thus boaters can use CB channels freely for social and personal messages; in many harbors launch services can only be called via CB. CB transceivers can be operated from shore in applications that are not available for VHF hand-held sets.

Currently, no FCC license is required for either a CB radio or its operator; no call signs are issued. There are, however, a few basic regulations that you should know and heed. Besides the distance limitations, output power must be no more than 4 watts carried on double-sideband transceivers and 12 watts peak power on SSB units. Sets for purchase conform to these limitations; do not add external amplifiers, which are available but illegal.

CB Channel 9—not to be confused with VHF Channel 9—is reserved for "emergency communications involving the immediate safety of life or the immediate protection of property." It is also available for "traveler assistance," but this is not defined in the FCC rules. Other CB channels are not restricted to any particular type of communications; the regulations designate no "calling and answering" frequency. All CB communications must be restricted to "the minimum practicable transmission time," but there are no specific limits between units of a single base station. Contacts between two different stations, however, must be limited to a maximum of five minutes, with no further transmission from either station for at least one minute following the end of their contact. These time limits do not apply in emergency situations.

CB communications can be in any language, but the FCC rules prohibit the use of codes (other than the "ten-code" operating signals). Communications with stations in foreign countries, other than Canada, are prohibited. The FCC regulations no longer require station identification, but such action is "encouraged." As no call signs are issued, you make up your own. Suggested forms include a CB call sign issued by the FCC before they stopped doing so, or "K" followed by your initials and the ZIP code for your home address. An organization name and assigned number is another alternative.

CB also may be used for voice paging. You may not use it to transmit music or sound effects. You may not receive any direct or indirect compensation for the use of your CB station, but this does not prevent the use of your CB set in connection with commercial services, provided you are paid for the services and not for the actual use of the CB equipment. You may not use your CB equipment to advertise or solicit the sale of goods or services. You must not use a CB set in any way to interfere intentionally with the operation of another station.

The full regulations governing the Citizens Band are found in Part 95 of the FCC Rules and Regulations.

## CB Equipment

Many CB transceivers used on boats are really designed and manufactured for use in cars and trucks. They are not built for a marine environment, but if properly protected from rain and spray, they will give good service for several years. CB sets especially built for marine service are a bit more expensive, but probably will turn out to be just as economical over a period of years, and they are likely to be more reliable.

CB transceivers must be "type accepted" by the FCC, and any repairs or modifications authorized by the manufacturer must be made by, or under the supervision of, a person "certified as technically qualified to perform transmitter installation, operation, maintenance, and repair duties in the private land mobile services and fixed services by an organization or committee representative of users in those services." You can install your set, and mount and adjust your antenna, but maintenance is limited to the replacement of fuses.

An antenna for a CB set on a boat must be specifically designed for such service; an antenna made for use on a vehicle will not operate satisfactorily. After installation of the set and antenna, a check should be made with an SWR meter designed for use on CB frequencies.

## Operating Your CB Radio

CB is not a "hobby" or a form of amateur radio to be operated for seeing how far, or with how many, different stations, you can talk. In some areas, local civil authorities or a CB club maintain a listening watch on CB 9 (or some other channel). If you install a CB set on your boat, find out who maintains a watch on Channel 9 in your area and make on-the-water tests with them to determine the range at which you can be heard.

No channel is assigned to any user or organization for their exclusive use; all users must share all channels. You will find, however, that certain types of users congregate on certain channels. Highway users are often found on Channel 19, boaters and fishermen on Channel 13 or some other locally adopted channel. There are no priorities except for emergencies, and such traffic will normally be handled on Channel 9. There is no "calling channel"—CB 9 is not like VHF 16 in this respect. Initial calls are normally made directly on the channel frequented by the category of stations with whom you wish to talk. There are no "Marine Operators" to connect you into the land telephone system.

# CHAPTER NINE

# AMATEUR RADIO

Amateur (ham) radio is an entirely separate service from marine radio communications, but it has many applications at sea, particularly for blue-water cruisers. Ham radio operates in frequency bands that extend lower and much higher than the dedicated marine frequencies—in a range from 1.8 to 24,000 MHz. Within these bands, many types of signals other than radiotelephone may be used—radiotelegraph (Morse), radioteletype, transponder relays via satellite. The interests of hams are wide, almost without limits.

### Getting a License

Amateur radio has its own license requirements; a VHF operator and station license does not allow you to establish or transmit on a ham station aboard your boat. A license is the first priority if you are considering having ham radio aboard.

Ham radio licenses are issued by the FCC in a series of grades that allow an increasing number of privileges as more advanced examinations are passed. Grades begin with Novice and progress through General and Advanced to Extra class. Outside of this progression but also available are the somewhat specialized Technician and proposed Communicator licenses. It is not necessary to start at the bottom. You may start at any level for which you can pass all the exam elements, and you can move up as rapidly as you wish and are able.

Most people start at the Novice level, which is enough to get you a call sign and limited operating privileges. One of the requirements for a Novice license is the ability to send and receive Morse code at a speed of five words a minute. This is not difficult and you can easily learn it from readily available practice cassette tapes. There is also a written examination on the rules of the amateur service, including relatively simple questions on amateur radio theory and procedures. Study guides are available to help you learn.

A Technician Class license may be obtained by passing a somewhat more advanced technical examination without increased code speed. It allows voice privileges on portions of VHF and UHF (ultra high frequency) bands, but not on the HF (high frequency) bands, where the longer-range boat-to-boat and boat-to-shore communications occur. For voice privileges on HF bands, you will need a General Class license, which requires a further written exam element and a 13-word-per-minute Morse code speed. The higher grades of licenses—Advanced and Extra—can follow if you wish to have operating privileges on certain special segments of the ham bands, but these are not necessary for effective communications from boats, and many hams stop at the General Class level.

A proposed new class of license—Communicator—would be the first "no-code" license ever created for U.S. hams. The written examination would be somewhat more technical than that presently required for a Technician/General license, and its operating privileges would be limited to 220 MHz and higher frequency bands. This would serve to introduce some people to ham radio, but would have little value for boaters. If and when it is established, there may be changes in the Novice and Technician classes.

You can obtain an amateur license by appearing before licensed amateurs who have been designated as Volunteer Examiners; it is not necessary to travel to an FCC office. Volunteer Examiners normally charge a small fee to cover expenses. There are no fees for license renewal or modification.

Many radio hams and clubs will gladly help a person desiring to qualify in amateur radio—that is one of the oldest traditions of the hobby. Information on locating such sources of help is available from stores selling ham equipment or by writing to the American Radio Relay League, Newington, CT 06111.

# About Ham Radio

Ham radio provides communications channels between boats, and between boats and shore stations, over short and long distances. All sorts of personal messages can be exchanged, but you cannot engage in business communications. Traditionally, hams have provided the first communications out of areas ravaged by natural disasters, such as hurricanes. There is no specified emergency channel, but there are several frequencies established by custom—among them 7.268 and 14.313 MHz—where there is someone listening nearly all the time. Many cruising craft at sea have obtained emergency help via ham radio. There is no service to marine telephone operators, but most shoreside ham operators will pass a message along, and some ham stations have the capability to "patch" a radio conversation into the telephone system. There are few restrictions on ham radio operations on boats, except when within the territorial waters of some foreign countries, particularly those where the telephone and telegraph services are owned by the government.

Amateur allocations in the radio spectrum are at 1.8, 3.5, 7.0, 10.1, 14.0, 18.068, 21.0, 24.89, and 28.0 MHz, plus segments in the VHF and UHF regions, and on up into microwaves. Communication distances in the ham bands will be roughly the same as for marine bands of approximately the same frequency. Although the regulations do require that the power used be kept to the minimum necessary, with a few exceptions, amateurs other than Novices can use up to 1,500 watts peak power.

# Equipment

Since essentially all equipment has solid-state components, most hams purchase their "rigs" from manufacturers, although some are assembled from kits. Equipment can be as inexpensive or as costly as the tastes and the budget of the buyer determine. A marine SSB or VHF transceiver can be used on the amateur bands if it covers those frequencies and can put out the type of signal used at those frequencies—some can and some can't. Conversely, though, an amateur transceiver is not type-accepted for marine-band service

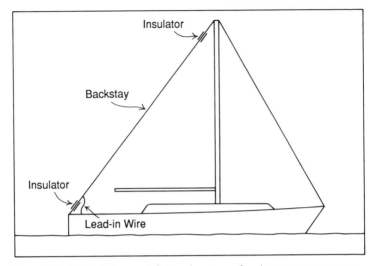

*Figure 9.1  Sailboats have a definite advantage when it comes to antennas for medium- and high-frequency radios, whether marine or amateur. Insulators placed near the top and bottom of a backstay enable that "wire" to be effectively used when connected through an antenna tuner.*

and cannot be so used. In general, a transceiver for amateur use has many more controls and is much more flexible in its operation. The design assumes some technical knowledge on the part of the operator; the set is susceptible to transmitting improper signals when used by an unqualified person.

**Antennas**

Small craft amateur radio antennas are generally similar to those used for marine SSB transceivers. Powerboats use a long whip, possibly with a center loading coil, and sailboats usually use an insulated backstay; both need an antenna tuner. If you use the 2-meter amateur band (144-148 MHz) for short-range contacts, the ham-radio antenna will closely resemble that used for VHF marine communications.

## Using Ham Radio

Ham radio is an excellent way to keep in touch with other boats and to coordinate cruising plans. Boats that are not equipped with marine SSB sets can use ham radio for longer-range communications. There are many "nets" that meet daily at designated times on specific frequencies. Even if you can't hear the other craft, there is usually someone who can relay for you. On some of these nets you can file "Position Reports" or "Float Plans" for your added safety as you cruise. The net will be expecting you to report at an appointed time and will alert authorities if you fail to do so. Also, your family can contact a local ham to pass along emergency messages via a net when you are away at sea. Remember, you must have a license to transmit, but you can monitor ham frequencies on your SSB receiver for messages. Or a friendly cruiser with a licensed ham station can receive messages and relay them to you via VHF marine radio.

The 2-meter ham band covers roughly the same distances and provides a medium for personal and social conversations that are not poper for marine VHF channels.

# CHAPTER TEN

# EMERGENCY POSITION-INDICATING RADIO BEACONS

L et 's start with one simple fact: an EPIRB may save your life if you have it on hand when you need it. It is an essential item of safety equipment for any vessel that goes beyond VHF range of shore stations and is not equipped with a medium frequency/high frequency SSB transceiver. It is a desirable item even if you do have an SSB on board, for the EPIRB can assist rescuers in finding you whether you are still on board or have abandoned ship and are in the water or on a life raft. There are several types of EPIRB; two—A and B—are most common, but they all have the same basic functions: to alert authorities, often through aircraft monitoring, to the fact that there is a vessel in trouble and to assist in locating it.

An EPIRB is a small radio transmitter that puts out an easily recognizable signal on certain frequencies; the frequencies vary with the type of EPIRB. It is closely related to an Emergency Locator Transmitter (ELT), which is carried in many aircraft. It is self-contained, with its own internal battery and antenna. It is either manually or automatically activated, depending upon the type.

Because an EPIRB transmits a radio signal, it must have an FCC license. The license is easily acquired by checking the appropriate box on the FCC license application, Form 506. If the EPIRB frequencies do not appear on your present license, it will be necessary to apply for a modified license using a Form 506 as before.

### About EPIRBs

Most EPIRBs are Class A or Class B units. The essential difference is that the "B" models must be activated manually. The "A" type will

*Figure 10.1 Emergency
Position Indicating
Radiobeacons (EPIRBs)
can be a vitally important
means of summoning
assistance in offshore
emergencies. Every craft
cruising outside of VHF
range should have one,
even if already equipped
with SSB radio.*

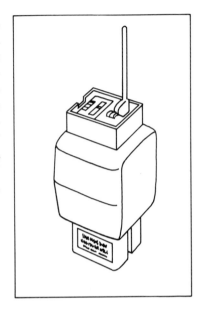

float free of a sinking vessel and then start transmitting automatically (these also have a switch for manual activation). The FCC rules require Class A EPIRBs on certain types of commercial vessels that operate more than three nautical miles offshore. Class A EPIRBs can also be carried on recreational craft, but the Class B model is more often used because of its lower cost. Both units transmit on 121.5 MHz, the emergency channel of civil aviation, and on 243 MHz, the "guard" channel for military aircraft. Aircraft are not required by law or regulation to monitor these frequencies, but many do. The EPIRB signal serves first to alert passing aircraft to the existence of an emergency, and subsequently to guide air and surface rescue units to the scene of distress. The transmitter is not powerful—less than 1 watt—but its signals can often be heard as far away as 200 miles by high-flying planes. If the signals are heard by more than one passing aircraft, it is frequently possible to get a very rough fix that will at least suggest the general area where detailed searching should begin.

There are now in orbit satellites of several nations that can receive

EPIRB signals and relay them to a ground station; many vessels have received assistance as a result of EPIRB signals picked up by a satellite. One limitation is that the satellite must simultaneously be within radio "vision" of both the source of the signals and a ground station. One or more kinds of modulation may be used; a chirping tone may be supplemented by a synthesized or prerecorded voice message beginning with "This is a recording."

A Class A EPIRB must float, and the base of the antenna must be a specified minimum distance above the surface of calm water. A Class B unit need not meet this requirement, but use of a flotation collar is advisable if the unit is not inherently buoyant.

FCC type approval requirements ensure that an EPIRB will operate continuously for at least 48 hours at rated power output, and many models will transmit even longer. Each battery is labeled with the date of manufacture and the date when 50 percent of its useful life will have expired. The battery must be replaced when this second date is reached or if the unit has been activated in an emergency.

### Using a Class A or B EPIRB

Although a Class A EPIRB will automatically start transmitting when it floats free of a sinking vessel, it is prudent to activate it manually as soon as it becomes evident that you may have to abandon ship. A Class B unit will, of course, have to be manually turned on. It is vitally important that once you have started your EPIRB you do NOT turn it off "to save the battery." You will not know when its signals have been picked up and the search begun; by turning it off you might miss opportunities for detection and/or seriously delay search operations. There are several verified cases where days were added to a search because of intermittent EPIRB signals.

An EPIRB must have a test switch for verifying the readiness of the unit. This may be activated for one second only during the first five minutes of any hour and do not do this at any other time. A very high percentage of EPIRB signals detected are false alarms, or result from other transmissions on or near the frequency, causing a considerable waste of time and money by the Coast Guard and other search and rescue resources. In one three-month period, the Coast

Guard received approximately 7,700 alerts on 121.5 MHz, of which only 220 were narrowed down to a definite location, and of these, only 14 involved a distress situation.

**Class S EPIRBs**

Class S EPIRBs are for use on survival craft, such as lifeboats and inflatable rafts. Coast Guard regulations require that they be carried on certain commercial vessels. They are generally similar to Class A models, but are manually activated only and may provide for either continuous or intermittent operation (approximately one minute on, one minute off). For vessels not required to carry a Class S EPIRB, a Class A or B unit may be used for the same purpose.

**Class C EPIRBs**

The FCC authorized a very different type of EPIRB in 1979 and units became available in 1981. The Class C device operates on VHF Channel 16 to alert other vessels and shore stations of an emergency situation, and on VHF Channel 15 to aid in the location of the distress. These units were to be used on boats on the Great Lakes and in coastal waters out to distances of roughly 20 miles from shore—the area covered by Coast Guard and other VHF shore stations. The goal was to have an EPIRB so inexpensive that boaters who did not equip their craft with VHF transceivers would carry this device to obtain emergency assistance. It didn't turn out that way—the cost of a Class C EPIRB is greater than that of the least-expensive models of VHF transceivers. It is not logical to pay more for a 1-watt signal, over which you can't talk about your troubles, than for a 25-watt set that provides full communication capabilities. The system still exists, and Class C EPIRBs are on the market, but few have been purchased and carried. It is likely that Class C EPIRBs will be phased out in the coming years.

**Categories 1 and 2 EPIRBS**

The latest development in EPIRBs are units that operate on 406.025 MHz and transmit signals to specially equipped satellites that are

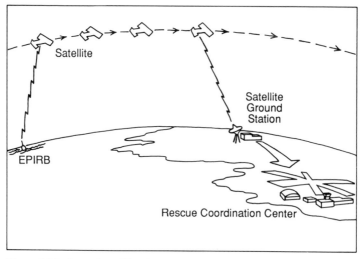

*Figure 10.2 Several satellites in space are equipped to receive and relay EPIRB signals, and more will be able to do so in future years. Signals from Class 1 and 2 EPIRBs can be stored on board for rebroadcast later as the satellite passes over one of its ground stations.*

capable of storing the signals after reception, and, if necessary, delaying retransmission until within range of a ground station. The new system provides the significant advantage of full coverage, eliminating the requirement that the satellite had to be simultaneously in view of the distressed vessel and a ground station. This is an international program and EPIRB transponders will be piggybacked on the satellites of several nations.

Category 1 and 2 EPIRBs correspond roughly to the older Class A and B models. The new units take advantage of advances in electronics since the design of the A and B 121.5/243.0 MHz versions. Both of the new types digitally transmit a serial number that, having been centrally recorded with the owner's name, address, telephone number, and the type of ship, will provide immediate identification of the vessel in distress. The new EPIRBs operate on 406.025 MHz but will also transmit on the old 121.5 MHz frequency for aircraft still listening to that frequency, and as an aid to rescue units searching by air or surface following the emergency alert on the higher frequency.

The EPIRBs in the new categories are currently (1990) considerably more expensive than the older models, but their prices can be expected to come down somewhat as the volume of production increases and development costs are amortized. The new models have already become Coast Guard-required equipment on certain types of commercial vessels, but will remain optional for recreational craft. If you put a Category 1 or 2 EPIRB on your boat, you must request modification of your station license to include the new frequency.

# CHAPTER ELEVEN

# CELLULAR TELEPHONES

ellular telephone service has become ubiquitous on land for private and commercial use in cars and trucks, but only recently has it gone to sea—a boon for those who need private, secure communication with the shore without the hassle of going through the VHF marine radiotelephone operator. Cellular phones are also useful when your vessel is tied up at a marina; your mobile unit can be used anywhere on the boat and takes the place of the traditional rented telephone with its umbilical cord to a dock connector.

You must remember, however, that insofar as safety afloat is concerned, a cellular telephone is not a substitute for a marine VHF radio.

## About Cellular Telephones

A cellular telephone is a cordless phone with a long range. Although it uses radio waves as its medium of communication, it offers all the services and features of an ordinary telephone. You can dial directly. You have your own seven-digit telephone number just as at home or work. Calls can be made directly to you. Special service features—call waiting, call forwarding, and so forth—are available on cellular phones. The sets themselves often have such features as a memory for frequently called numbers, last number redial, an indicator of calls that came in while you were away from the phone, volume control, and back-lighted number pad. These units also can be interfaced to alarm systems and will call preset numbers in case of fire, taking on water, break-ins, or other problems.

A VHF public correspondence station—Marine Operator—may

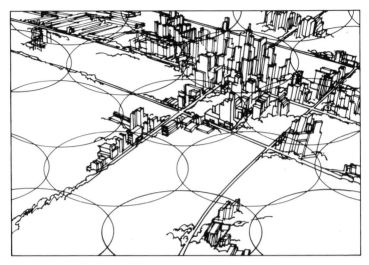

*Figure 11.1  The cellular telephone service provides excellent service by dividing its coverage area into numerous "cells," each with its own receiver, transmitter, and sets of frequency pairs. A central computer tracks the signals from users and switches from one cell to another as required.*

have one receiving and transmitting antenna, or perhaps two or three for better coverage; these stations operate on the same channel (or channels) on all antennas. A cellular system, on the other hand, has many receiving/transmitting locations in a series of cells, with each cell transmitting on its own pair of frequencies. When you are communicating on a cellular system, you will be using the cell that receives your signal best, usually the one in which you are located. As your location changes, the cell that you use changes so that communications continue at full quality. The changes are made automatically through a central computer; the shifts between cells are not noticeable in voice transmissions; they may, however, cause a brief gap in data transmissions. Adjacent cells use different frequency pairs, but because of the low power of these transmitters, pairs may be reused in the more distant cells of a system, and in other systems. As traffic increases, the size of individual cells can be reduced and more cells added.

## Cellular Telephones for Your Boat

There are now available, but at higher cost, cellular phones designed for operation in marine environments of moisture, corrosion, and vibration. But most cellular telephones used on boats are adapted from units designed and marketed for cars and trucks. There are models that can be built in; there are transportable units powered by a rechargeable battery that can be moved from one location to another boat, and there are hand-held models very much like a cordless telephone for your home.

A transportable unit that can be used from either your car or your boat is obviously more economical than having two separate units. Some "fixed" units can become transportable with an optional modification kit. It is important to remember, however, that cellular telephones designed for use in cars are probably not as water resistant as marine radios and so will require a more protected location on your craft.

Transportable units usually have an attached antenna, but for best results from your boat make sure that you can detach this antenna and connect a cable that runs to one that is mounted in a higher and clearer location. Ranges of 10 or so miles over water are normal, with greater distances occasionally being reached. Transportables operate from an integral battery pack that can be recharged from either a 120-V AC outlet or the 12-V DC system of a car or boat. Recharge time can vary from one to five hours depending upon the charger that you are using. The unit also can be "floated" on the vehicle's power system so that power is not taken from the battery and it remains fully charged.

Hand-held cellular phones, often called "portable" units, operate at a lower power level, usually 0.6 watts, but they can be connected to an installed antenna through an external power amplifier that will boost the output to the legal maximum of 3 watts. Hand-held units are powered by a smaller internal battery than those used with transportable models. Operating time for portable units may be as little as 45 minutes on the air, with several hours of stand-by receive time. Batteries are easily changed, and you should carry a spare.

# Selecting Your Equipment

There are two steps in getting started—buying the equipment and signing up with an operating service. In any of the 306 cellular phone geographic areas in the United States there are, by FCC rules, two competing cellular services. One is the regular telephone ("wire-line") company and the other an independent ("non-wire-line") organization. Each service can support several hundred thousand subscribers. In nearly all cases, the price quoted for a cellular phone is contingent upon your signing up for service with a specific system.

Ask specifically about the location of cells adjacent to your boating area and how far out from shore you can expect coverage (it may not be as far as VHF Marine Operator service). Ask to see charts of antenna locations and coverage diagrams. Then there is the matter of "roaming agreements" with your home-city company; these cover the use of your cellular phone when you are in areas serviced by other systems. If you cruise to other areas, coverage by roaming agreements is essential for continued cellular service from your craft. (Because cellular systems operate in the ultrahigh frequency (UHF) band at low power levels, the frequency pairs used in one area can be reused in other areas, so that your phone can work in many locations.) Cellular phone service is now available in some cruising areas, such as the Bahamas and the British Virgin Islands, where antennas on high points of land extend service far out to sea.

Having selected your system, look for the best deal on the phone itself. There are many brands, models, and dealers, and there will be differences in special features. Initially, cellular phones had a 666 channel capacity, but this has now been increased to 832; an older model may meet your needs at a lower cost. Most units have the capability of holding in memory frequently called numbers, a considerable operating convenience, but the capacity of the memory will vary among models. Cellular phones have a small LCD display that will show many items of information; pick a unit that will give you the information that you need. Many sets will show in the display the number that you are calling. Some models will indicate that calls were made to you while you were away from your set and even show the telephone numbers of the callers. Some models will even record a brief message that can be read later. On some models you can talk to the phone and tell it what number you want dialed!

If you expect to transmit data from your cellular phone via modem, make sure that your unit has an RJ-11 jack into which you can connect a line—this is similar to the modular wall jack now used widely for telephones in homes and offices. This jack also can be used for interfacing an alarm system. Another jack for the connection of a louder signaling device may be desirable for use of your phone in a noisy environment, such as a performance-type powerboat.

A marine antenna may be as small as the short curlicue ones used on cars, or it may be as long as a 6-dB VHF antenna. Whatever the size, mount it as high as possible and in the clear from other antennas or metal structures. Good-quality cable should be used to avoid any excessive loss of the 3-watt or less signal. A new antenna that will soon be available requires no cable. An SWR check after installation is desirable, but the meter must be suitable for use at the UHF cellular frequencies.

## Using Your Cellular Phone Afloat

There are no "operating procedures" for cellular telephones; you use one just as you would a regular phone in your home or office. Just pick the phone up from its holder, listen for a dial tone, and punch in your number.

### Costs

While the prices of cellular phones have come down dramatically since they were introduced a few years ago—from thousands of dollars to several hundred—there always seem to be sales, so shopping around can save money. But there are also costs for having the service available and for each use of it. The monthly access charge will vary from area to area and company to company, but it averages about $30. Charges for calls are based on "air time" at about 30 to 40¢ per minute in "peak" time, less in "off-peak" hours.

You pay this for *both* outgoing and incoming calls. You may have a choice of several service plans based on varying monthly charges and anticipated amounts of use. Special features, such as Call Waiting, Call Forwarding, etc., are charged separately.

When you use your cellular phone outside your home area under roaming agreements, dialing procedures and charges will be different and will vary from place to place. It is possible in some areas to have calls originating in your home city forwarded automatically. In other areas, you must first dial the "roamer access number" for the area to which you have roamed. Long-distance charges apply for forwarded calls. Procedures and charges are spelled out in detail in booklets prepared by the service companies. If you anticipate using a cellular phone while cruising, it is advisable to compare the services and charges of the two providers before signing up.

**Added Features**

A cellular-telephone installation provides only one instrument. On larger yachts, this means that the phone will often not be where you are when you want to use it. You can get around this limitation by installing a small and inexpensive interface unit that will permit you to tie the cellular phone into any on-board telephone system that you have installed. With this interconnection, you can receive and place calls from any telephone on your craft.

Additionally, or alternatively, you can use a cordless phone in a manner similar to the way you would use one in your home. Thus, with the base unit at the cellular-telephone installation, you can receive or place calls from any place around your boat, or even from the pier or a nearby craft as long as you are within the range limitation of the cordless phone.

With an interfacing unit, called an RJ-11 adapter, you can also connect a fax machine or a modem for your personal computer. Although not absolutely necessary, an automatic switch can be installed that will sense the nature of an incoming call and switch it to the telephone, fax machine, or modem, as appropriate. In voice communications you will normally not notice a shift between cells; with data reception and transmission there may be a detectable, but very brief, interruption in the flow of data—this is rarely a problem.

# CHAPTER TWELVE

# SATELLITE COMMUNICATIONS

C ommunication via satellite (SatCom) is probably the most expensive way of transmitting and receiving information between two points, which is why at sea it has been limited to commercial and military vessels. Despite some decreases in cost, SatCom is still prohibitive for anything but the largest mega-power yachts. A SatCom dome containing a dish antenna is hardly ever seen on a sailing vessel, because it will not function while the boat is heeling, although there are now means of compensating for the angle. Yet a boat equipped with a SatCom dome is what the FCC calls a Ship Earth Station (SES), and for maritime communication it affords many options. It can handle two-way exchanges of voice, telex, facsimile, and data. Communications are extremely reliable, of the highest quality, and secure from interception. Distress messages are automatically routed directly to regional rescue coordination centers. Although far more expensive than their nearest relative—SSB—for those who must have such a capability, satellite communications are independent of weather and instantly available worldwide.

## The INMARSAT System

The International Maritime Satellite Organization (InMarSat) is a cooperative venture of more than 55 nations to coordinate and control the use of three satellites in geosynchronous orbit above the equator—one each for the Atlantic, Pacific, and Indian oceans, and adjacent land areas. ("Geosynchronous" means that, although the satellites are moving at great speeds through space, their movement is matched to the rotation of the earth, so that they appear to be always in the same location.) The ground terminals are called coast earth stations (CES); there are roughly 25 of them located throughout the world. The United States section of Inmarsat is operated by Comsat Maritime Services and is regulated by the FCC.

### Standard A Equipment

The first generation of maritime satellite communication systems uses equipment that is described as Standard A or Standard C. Standard A is what you see on large yachts and ships today. Standard A provides the most complete communications services—telephone, facsimile, telex, and data transfer at various transmission speeds, including slow-scan TV images. A complete installation can cost tens of thousands of dollars, but for those who need the services, it may be worth it.

Standard A equipment includes a spherical dome housing a dish antenna, roughly one meter (3+ feet) in diameter. Because of the movement of the vessel, the antenna must be motor-driven to keep its very high-gain, very sharp beam constantly pointed toward the satellite. This requires input from a gyrocompass for heading direction and motion detectors to sense changes in roll and pitch; these requirements constitute a major part of the complexity and cost of the station.

Within the vessel will be one or more units containing much of the electronics for the ship station; portions of the transmitter and receiver are in the dome with the antenna.

### Standard C Equipment

For vessels that have no room for a large and heavy Standard A antenna installation, and vessel owners who cannot afford the costs, there is the newer Standard C. There is, of course, a reduction in the capabilities of such a set. Voice cannot be used, and data is handled at a reduced rate, effectively 600 bits per second. Messages are entered into the system from a computer keyboard or telex terminal. They are transmitted in a way similar to that of the Standard A system—up to

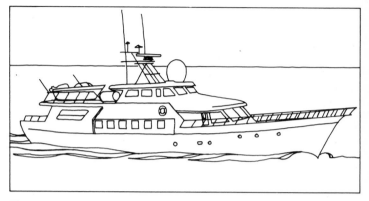

*Figure 12.1 Yachts can be equipped for satellite communications and use voice, teletype, facsimile, data, and slow-scan TV. The Standard A terminal antenna is relatively large and is suitable only for larger craft and ships.*

a satellite and back down to a coast earth station where they are put into the land communications network for delivery. Traffic inbound to the ship travels the same route in reverse.

A Standard C station uses a much smaller and lighter antenna that is omnidirectional and need not be constantly steered to keep the satellite in sight. The electronics package below-decks is also less complex, smaller, lighter, and less expensive. A complete installation will presently run from $12,000 to $15,000. If receive-only equipment will meet your needs, the cost can be reduced from one-third to one-half of that amount.

## Using Satellite Communications

Making a telephone call from a Standard A ship station is essentially the same as phoning from your home or office. You must start with a code number that tells the satellite to which coast station you wish your call routed. For U.S. and Canadian calls, this is followed by the normal area code and local telephone number. Calls can be direct-dialed without operator intervention, or a two-digit prefix can be added for person-to-person, collect, or other special service calls.

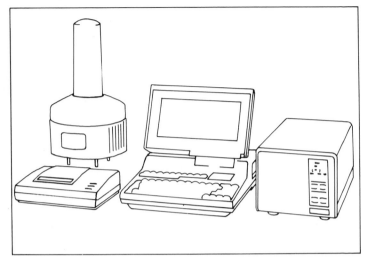

*Figure 12.2 A more recent development in maritime satellite communications is the "Standard C" equipment, with antennas small enough for installation on almost any boat. Voice cannot be used, but data communications and telex are available.*

Calls go through directly, and probably the persons on the other end will not know how you are calling unless you tell them!

Telex and other data communications likewise go through automatically with a minimum of additional procedures. Position data from a radionavigation system, such as Loran or GPS, can be interfaced into the SatCom equipment for automatic transmittal without manual entry. (After dialing a number, press # for a voice call, or press + for a telex call.)

Incoming phone calls and data transmissions from on shore can sometimes be put through without the services of an operator, using an "ocean code" in place of country and city codes. Calls via satellite also can be made from one vessel to another.

Communications through a Standard C ship station follow similar procedures, subject to limitations of the types of traffic that can be sent and received.

Both systems have certain special features. Group Calling allows the same message to go out simultaneously to a number of specified ship stations. Typical of such calls are transmissions of weather, navigational hazards, and similar data to all vessels in or approaching a defined geographic area. Fleet-type group calls can provide communications to a designated group of vessels, such as those of a commercial operation. SeaMail™ is a form of electonic mailbox service where messages can be left for later retrieval by the addressee; access codes ensure privacy. Daily summaries of news, sports, and financial information are broadcast by telex on regular schedules. The U.S. Armed Forces Radio and Television Service now uses satellites instead of shortwave radio to reach military bases around the globe. SatCom-equipped vessels can listen in for news, play-by-play descriptions of major sport events, and other features.

For larger private vessels, YachtPhone equipment provides voice, facsimile, and computer communications service to multiple on-board locations, functioning much like a conventional internal telephone system in an office onshore.

With some ship earth station equipment, an interface capability will enable nearby vessels to communicate first by VHF radio to the ship and then beyond by SatCom.

# Future Developments in SatCom

While Standard A and Standard C are the major SatCom systems working today, there are plans to develop better services. Standard B will be a technological advancement and improvement on Standard A; data transmission rates will be increased and several specialized telephone services will be added.

Standard M is an advancement from Standard C that allows telephone communications and higher data speeds (though still not as fast as Standard A) while retaining a small, lightweight, omnidirectional antenna. As technology advances, and as more sets are produced, prices will likely come down, though to what level cannot be predicted. And, as in the past with VHF and Loran C, the gear will become smaller. At least one electronics company, for instance, has announced a multisatellite "pocket telephone" system.

# CHAPTER THIRTEEN

# VISUAL AND SOUND COMMUNICATIONS

The use of visual signals between vessels, and between a vessel and the shore, must surely go back to the earliest days of man's travels on the water. Radio is now the dominant means of communications, but it is by no means the only method. It is often desirable to supplement or even replace radio communications with sight and sound.

### The Value of Visual Communications

Visual signaling should not be a new or unfamiliar idea to a small-craft skipper, even though he or she may lack the knowledge to read such signals. Acquiring a basic knowledge of visual communications can be of value to a boater in at least two ways. Merchant ships will be flying signal flags indicating the presence of a pilot on board, the handling of dangerous cargoes, or an imminent departure. Navy and Coast Guard vessels probably will be flying many more flags. Knowing the meaning of at least some of these will give a boater a greater sense of belonging to the maritime world.

The greater value in a knowledge of signaling, however, lies in the added margin of safety that it can provide. So much dependence is placed today on a boat's radiotelephone that one often overlooks the possibility of its not being available when most needed. The cause need not be an electronic failure; it can merely be the lack of a common frequency or mode of modulation. Although radio will undoubtedly remain your primary means of communication, do not overlook the possibilities of visual signaling.

# The International Code of Signals

The International Code of Signals is published in the United States as DMAHTC *Publication No. 102*. It may be bought from some local sales agents who sell charts and navigational publications, or by mail from the Government Printing Office, Washington, DC, or regional GPO Bookstores.

*Pub. 102* includes both general procedures applicable to all forms of communication and specific rules for flag-hoist signaling, flashing-light signaling, sound signaling, and signaling by hand-held flags using either semaphore or Morse code. The publication also gives some procedures for radiotelephony.

The signals listed in *Pub. 102* consist of: (1) single-letter signals allocated to messages that are very urgent or important, or which are in very common use; (2) two-letter signals for general messages; and (3) three-letter signals (all beginning with the letter "M") for medical messages.

"Complements"—numerals following a basic two-letter signal—are added to certain signals to express: (1) variations in the meaning of the basic signal; (2) questions and answers relating to the meaning of the basic signal; or (3) supplementary, specific, or more detailed meanings.

### Typical Code Signals

The single-letter, basic signals are not limited to flags; they can be sent by any form of communication. Typical two-letter signal groups are listed in Figure 13.1.

### Special Procedures

When you send names, or other words for which there are no signal groups in the International Code, they must be spelled out. The signal group "YZ" may be used to indicate that the groups that follow are plain language rather than code groups. You can, however, omit this indicator if the spelling is obvious.

The International Code provides special time-saving procedures for many purposes, such as signaling time, courses and bearings, and geographic coordinates. (Details are given in *Pub. No. 102.*)

The Code is truly international—meanings have been established in nine languages. This results in some complications, and specific procedures given in *Pub. No. 102* must be followed to avoid erroneous interpretations of the signals you send out. Read that publication carefully before attempting to use the Code.

## Flag Hoist Signaling

A complete set of International Code flags consists of the 26 alphabetical flags, 10 numeral pennants, three "substitutes" (the Navy has four), and the answering pennant. Substitute pennants (the Navy calls them "repeaters") serve as replacements for flags or pennants already used in a hoist; each set has only one of each flag and pennant.

Five standardized colors are used as signal flags: red, white, blue, yellow, and black. On most of the flags two colors, selected for maximum contrast, are combined. Two flags are of a single solid color; several use three colors; and one uses four colors. Stripes and simple shapes are used to get enough clearly distinguishable patterns to provide for the number of characters involved. Each flag and pennant has a length of line sewn into its hoist edge, extending above the cloth to a ring and a short distance below the bottom to a snap hook. This "tail-line" provides spacing between adjacent flags of a hoist. The use of rings and snaps allows the rapid joining of the individual flags and pennants, and their connection to a signal halyard. There is also a "tackline," a piece of line having a ring and snap hook but no cloth flag; it is used as a spacer in a hoist.

Signal flags can be flown singly or in combinations of two or more; flags and pennants can be mixed as required. Probably the most often seen single-flag signals will be "B" on vessels handling dangerous cargoes (fuel or explosives) and "H" on vessels with a pilot on board.

| AE | I must abandon my vessel. |
| CJ | Do you require assistance? |
| CO | I am unable to give assistance. |
| JI | Are you aground? |
| JL | You are running the risk of going aground |
| JW | I have sprung a leak. |
| KN | I cannot take you in tow. |
| LN | Light (name follows) has been extinguished. |
| LO | I am not in my correct position. (To be used by a lightship.) |
| LR | Bar is not dangerous |
| LS | Bar is dangerous |
| MF | Course to reach me is . . . |
| MG | You should steer course . . . |
| NF | You are running into danger. |
| NG | You are in a dangerous position. |

*Figure 13.1  Various single letters and combinations of two and three letters are used for signaling with flag hoists, flashing light, and other methods. Shown here are typical two-letter code groups that are of general interest.*

**General Yachting Use of Signal Flags**

Some boats carry a full set of signal flags. Most do not; but they probably carry one or more flags that are used in their day-to-day operations. Here are some of them:

*The "Q" Flag.* The flying of the single "Q" flag when entering a foreign port or returning to a U.S. port from a voyage that has taken you into foreign waters is in accordance with its International Code meaning "My vessel is healthy and I request free practique." (*Practique* is the formal term for permission to use a port.) The flag signifies that the vessel has not yet cleared with customs and immigration authorities; take it down when you have completed clearance.

*The "T" Flag.* There are several single-letter signals informally used in yachting that do not appear in the International Code. The code flag "T," often seen on boats at yacht clubs and marinas where moorings are used, is a request for transportation—a call for the launch serving the moorings to come and pick up passengers for the shore or another craft.

*The "M" Letter.* Another unofficial signal, "M" is flown to indicate a boat that has a medical doctor on board; again this differs from the International Code meaning. This signal is not yet in widespread use, but its value is recognized and it is being seen on more and more boats; knowledge that there is a doctor in the area can be of considerable importance in the event of an accident.

*"A" Flag.* This is the official notification of a diver nearby, even though the informal red field with white slash is used more often today.

**The International Morse Code**

The International Morse Code of dots and dashes can be used for signaling by flashes of light or bursts of sound, as well as by radiotelegraphy. Morse code letters, numerals, and punctuation marks are signaled by combinations of dots and dashes. Letters have from one to four components, numerals have five, and punctuation marks have six. The basic Morse code is shown in Figure 13.2. The dots, dashes, and the spaces between them are defined in terms of units—a dot is one unit and a dash is three units. The space between the dots and/or dashes of a single character is one unit, the space between characters is three units, and the space between words or code groups is five units. The length of any unit is set by the skill of the sending operator and the mode of signaling being used. You should transmit only as fast as you can do so smoothly and accurately. And don't send faster than you can receive; your sending speed may well guide the other operator's speed in sending to you. If in doubt, slow down and slightly exaggerate the length of the dashes and spaces rather than shorten them.

**Flashing-Light Signaling**

Although boaters have little use for flashing-light signaling in normal operations, this means of communications can be valuable in emergency situations. Take, for example, the case of a boat aground at night without a radio, or with one that is inoperative. It may be unsafe for another craft to approach close enough for shouting back and forth across the gap between them. There may be uncertainty as to where the shoal water lies, or the other vessel may draw considerably more water and thus have to stand off at a distance. Knowledge of the Morse code and the possession of a light with which to signal may save the day.

Flashing-light signaling has the advantage of requiring no special equipment—an ordinary flashlight or electric lantern may be readily used. A searchlight can be used, but you should use a solid object to act as a shutter and interrupt the light into dots and dashes; don't try to signal by switching the light on and off.

# Semaphore Signaling

This may be thought of as a "Boy Scout" activity, but it has long been used between naval vessels. A pair of hand-held, colorful flags is usually used for increased visibility. Over short distances, the flags can be omitted, but the use of handkerchiefs or rags will aid in the reading of the signals. Semaphore signaling is very satisfactory for day use, but it requires the learning of a new code (or perhaps the refreshing of old knowledge) plus regular use and practice to reach any degree of proficiency. See Figure 13.3.

Even if a boater is not qualified in semaphore signaling, a knowledge of the letter "R" is often useful. "R" has wide recognition as "Roger" on radiotelephone circuits, meaning "received and understood." The semaphore "R"—both arms stretched out horizontally to the sides—is a simple yet fully effective way of signaling to another person that you "got the message." Clearly and distinctly given, it is a much more satisfactory means of acknowledging information or instructions than a careless wave of one hand.

# The International Morse Code

| | | | | | |
|---|---|---|---|---|---|
| A | • — | M | — — | Y | — • — — |
| B | — • • • | N | — • | Z | — — • • |
| C | — • — • | O | — — — | 1 | • — — — — |
| D | — • • | P | • — — • | 2 | • • — — — |
| E | • | Q | — — • — | 3 | • • • — — |
| F | • • — • | R | • — • | 4 | • • • • — |
| G | — — • | S | • • • | 5 | • • • • • |
| H | • • • • | T | — | 6 | — • • • • |
| I | • • | U | • • — | 7 | — — • • • |
| J | • — — — | V | • • • — | 8 | — — — • • |
| K | — • — | W | • — — | 9 | — — — — • |
| L | • — • • | X | — • • — | 0 | — — — — — |

Period     • — • — • —
Comma     — — • • — —
Interrogative   • — •   — — • —   (RQ)
Distress Call   • • • — — — • • •   (SOS)
From     — • •   •   (DE)
Invitation to transmit (go ahead)    — • —   (K)
Wait     • — • • •   (AS)
Error     • • • • • • • •   (EEEE etc.)
Received    • — •   (R)
End of each message   • — • — •   (AR)

A dash is equal to three dots.
The space between parts of the same letter is equal to one dot.
The space between two letters is equal to three dots.
The space between two words is equal to five dots.

*Figure 13.2 It takes a bit of effort and patience to learn the Morse code, but it is worth it, and occasional use will keep it in your mind for life. It can be used to communicate by radio, audible sound, and flashing light; in many situations it may be essential for your safety.*

# External Sound Communications

There will often be occasions requiring voice communications over short distances where the use of radio is impractical or undesirable. The human voice carries very well over water, but there is often engine noise or wind from the wrong direction when your unamplified voice just isn't sufficient; or perhaps you can't get close enough to an aground or disabled vessel. What you need is a Loud Hailer, (normally called just a "hailer") to amplify your voice.

### About Hailers

Many models of VHF and CB radios have a set of terminals on the back panel marked "hailer" or "PA System." These provide for the use of the set's audio amplifier for external purposes, but the power level is only that of the set's normal radio receiver, roughly two to five watts, and is not sufficient to serve effectively as a hailer.

Several manufacturers market electronic devices specifically designed as hailers. These have power outputs of roughly 20 to 30 watts, sufficient for all normal applications. Make sure that the speaker that you plan to use can handle the power level of your amplifier without excess distortion.

A valuable feature of most hailers is the capacity to "listen back," with the speaker serving as a microphone to pick up the voice of the person answering you. This "two-way" function will extend the range at which information and directions can be passed back and forth. It will also enable you to detect fog signals, or breakers on the rocks, at greater and safer distances.

Hailers for boats come with several special features. They can generate an audio tone used as a fog signal that can be operated manually or automatically at preset intervals. (The maximum interval is now the same in all waters; don't be misled by such markings as "International," or "Inland." The signals themselves, however, vary with the vessel and the situation; be sure to sound the proper signal for your craft and circumstances.)

A hailer can also serve as an internal intercom system and can be

*Figure 13.3 Semaphore signaling relies on two small flags held in a variety of positions, each of which communicates a letter; if proper flags are not available, any sort of colorful cloth, or even bare hands, can be used. This can be very useful over short distances.*

interfaced with music systems, alarm sensors, and even VHF or CB radios. Some models can produce an alarm signal often described as a "yelp."

### Installation

A hailer is usually about the size and shape of a VHF radio. It should be installed so that it is convenient to the helm position, but exercise caution over its distance from the steering compass, for the internal speaker has a strong magnet similar to that of a VHF or CB radio. The hailer's power requirements will be up to 10 amperes at 12 volts DC; check the manual of your unit for the proper sizes of wire and fuse. Be sure to twist all power leads that come anywhere near a compass.

The hailer's speaker must be carefully sited to be most effective. If the speaker horn is rectangular, it must be properly oriented since sound is more concentrated in one plane than the other. If the horn is fixed in position, as it usually is, you want the broader distribution of sound in the horizontal plane, for the speaker will not always be pointed directly at the intended listener, especially in storm-tossed seas.

An interesting alternative mounting of a hailer's speaker is on a mount that can be rotated about horizontal and vertical axes like a searchlight (or on the searchlight itself). This provides the most effectively "aimed" sound to listeners, with the best possibility of hearing their replies via the "listen-back" feature. Even more valuable is the capability of a speaker thus mounted to use the hailer's listening function as an "audio direction finder." It can give you a surprisingly accurate indication of the relative bearing of a fog signal. Or you can orient the horn directly forward and "home in" on the fog signal, but keep a sharp lookout and don't run into it.

### Hand-held Power Megaphones

An alternative or supplement to an installed hailer is a Power Megaphone. This is a microphone, amplifier, speaker, and battery in one unit. Its power output will be less than that of most hailers, but its ability to project sound directly toward the intended recipient does much to make up for this deficiency. Such units normally have a microphone volume control, but usually do not have a "listen-back" capability.

# CHAPTER FOURTEEN

# ON-BOARD
# COMMUNICATIONS

F or both safety and convenience there are Internal Communications requirements on most boats. The individual at the helm, for instance, must be able to communicate directly with persons below decks, or on deck but too far away to hear adequately, without leaving the helm for even the briefest moment. He or she may simply be calling for food or drink, but might also be calling for immediate assistance in a sudden emergency.

A special need for on-board communications arises when anchoring or mooring a boat, or during docking. Engine noise, strong winds, thunder, and so forth, may make calling back and forth from the bow to the helm station impossible or unreliable. Solutions can include either a forward intercom station or a set of hand signals.

### On-Board Hand Signals

Hand Signals are especially useful between a person at the helm and a person lowering an anchor or picking up a mooring pennant. There are no established sets of signals for this purpose, and each crew must work up its own method. The signals must be simple and unmistakable. They should be easily learned by all who may have occasion to use them. Signals should cover all possible situations and commands; they should be reviewed and revised as often as necessary.

### External Hand Signals

Hand signals can also be used for communicating to others not on your boat. It is important that you know and use a standard set of signals, as there often will not be an opportunity for the people signaling to learn together the meanings of the various gestures.

### Signals for Water Skiing

The following set of signals has been approved by the American Water Ski Association. The signals are simple and often obvious, but before using them in an actual skiing situation, be sure that the skier, the observer, and the boat operator all know and understand these signals.

- Faster—Palm of one hand pointing upward.
- Slower—Palm of one hand pointing downward.
- Speed—One arm raised, with thumb and index finger joined to form a circle.
- Right Turn—Arm outstretched, pointing to the right.
- Left Turn—Arm outstretched, pointing to the left.
- Return to the Drop-Off Area—Arm held at 45° angle from body, pointing downward and swinging.
- Cut Motor—Finger drawn across throat.
- Stop—Hand up, palm forward.
- Skier OK After Fall—Hands clenched together overhead.
- Pick Me Up or Fallen Skier, Watch Out—One ski held up vertically out of the water.

### Hand Signals for Towing Situations

A special use for hand signals occurs when your boat is towing another or being towed, or when you are trying to pull off a craft that has run aground (or when yours is the boat aground and in need of a pull!). Direct contact by VHF radio is, of course, the preferred means of communication, but this is not always possible; one of the boats may not have a radio, or may have a dead battery. Here, hand signals are essential, at least for minimal communications.

Since two boats are involved and the persons concerned are most likely strangers to one another, a standard set of signals must be

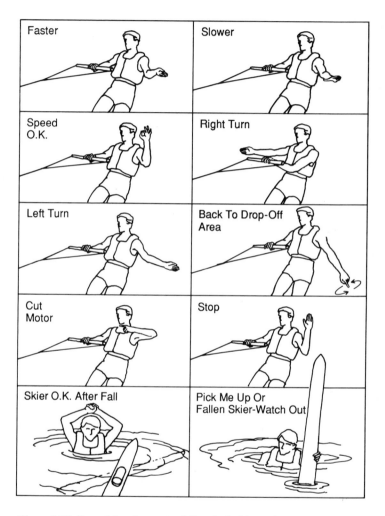

*Figure 14.1 For safety when waterskiing, both skier and operator or observer should know this set of hand signals.*

used; they must be simple and have obvious meanings.

*Tow line attached.* Towing must never start until the line is securely fastened on the craft to be towed; the fastening cannot always be seen clearly from the towing craft and must be specifically signalled from the disabled boat before a strain is taken on the line. The signal for this is both arms raised over the head with the hands clasped together—the gesture commonly used to signify victory in a contest or athletic event.

*Start pulling.* This signal normally follows soon after the one above, but also may be needed after any pause or interruption in the pulling process. One arm is raised above the head and rotated in small circles with the index finger extended—this is similar to the signal used by persons directing the work of a crane operator to indicate taking up on the hook.

*Signals for speed changes.* The skipper of a towing vessel may not be able to judge adequately the effects of speed on the towed craft. A person on the latter boat can signal a decrease in speed by extending both arms out horizontally, hands open with palms down, and then moving his arms downward and back to horizontal several times. This is the same as the signal often used when another boat goes by you too fast and you wish it to slow down. Conversely, if the towed vessel wishes to signal an increase in speed, the arms can be extended as before, but with the palms up, and then moved upward and back to horizontal several times.

*Stop or wait.* A need to interrupt operations can be signaled from either boat by a person holding up one arm with an open palm facing the other craft (the signal used by traffic police to indicate that an approaching vehicle should stop).

*Finished.* When the towing or pulling task is completed, and it is desired that the line between the boats be cast off, a signal can be made from either boat, when appropriate. This is done by bringing both hands together at waist level and extending them out to each side, repeated several times. Football fans will recognize this as the same as the signal for an incomplete forward pass.

# APPENDICES

## Appendix A
## Marine VHF Channel Assignments in U.S. Waters

| Channel Number | Frequency (MHz) Transmit | Recieve | Communications Purpose |
|---|---|---|---|
| 01A | 156.050 | 156.050 | Port Operations; Commercial Intership & Ship-to-Coast[1] |
| 05A | 156.250 | 156.250 | Port Operations; Intership & Ship-to-Coast[2] |
| 06 | 156.300 | 156.300 | Intership- Safety only; USCG Search & Rescue |
| 07A | 156.350 | 156.350 | Commercial- Intership & Ship-to-Coast |
| 08 | 156.400 | 156.400 | Commercial- Intership |
| 09 | 156.450 | 156.450 | Commercial & Non-commercial- Intership & Ship to Coast |
| 10 | 156.500 | 156.500 | Commercial- Intership & Ship-to-Coast |
| 11 | 156.550 | 156.550 | Commercial- Intership & Ship-to-Shore[1] |
| 12 | 156.600 | 156.600 | Port Operations- Intership & Ship-to-Shore[3] |
| 13 | 156.650 | 156.650 | Navigation- Bridge-to-Bridge[4] |
| 14 | 156.700 | 156.700 | Port Operations- Intership & Ship-to-Coast[3] |

| Channel Number | Frequency (MHz) Transmit | Recieve | Communications Purpose |
|---|---|---|---|
| 15 | NA | 156.750 | Environmental Information (Receive only)[5] |
| 16 | 156.800 | 156.800 | Distress, Safety, and Calling and Answering[5] |
| 17 | 156.850 | 156.850 | Maritime Control Great Lakes weather & Safety info[6] |
| 18A | 156.900 | 156.900 | Commercial- Intership & Ship-to-Coast |
| 19A | 156.950 | 156.950 | Commercial- Intership & Ship-to-Coast |
| 20 | 157.000 | 157.000 | Port Operations- Intership & Ship-to-Coast |
| 21A | 157.050 | 157.050 | *U.S. Government Use Only*-(USCG internal working channel) |
| 22A | 157.100 | 157.100 | USCG Liaison & Working Channel- Marine Safety Broadcasts |
| 23A | 157.150 | 157.150 | *U.S. Government Use Only*- (USCG internal working channel) |
| 24 | 156.200 | 161.800 | Public Correspondence- (Marine Operator) |
| 25 | 156.250 | 161.850 | Public Correspondence- (Marine Operator) |
| 26 | 156.300 | 161.900 | Public Correspondence- (Marine Operator) |
| 27 | 156.350 | 161.950 | Public Correspondence- (Marine Operator) |
| 28 | 156.400 | 162.000 | Public Correspondence- (Marine Operator) |
| 63A | 156.175 | 156.175 | Port Operations; Commercial- Intership & Ship-to-Coast[1] |
| 65A | 156.275 | 156.275 | Port Operations- Intership & Ship-to-Coast |
| 66A | 156.325 | 156.325 | Port Operations- Intership & Ship-to-Coast |
| 67 | 156.375 | 156.375 | Navigational- Bridge-to-Bridge[7] |
| 68 | 156.425 | 156.425 | Non-commercial- Intership & Ship-to-Coast |

| Channel Number | Frequency (MHz) Transmit | Recieve | Communications Purpose |
|---|---|---|---|
| 69 | 156.475 | 156.475 | Non-commercial-Intership & ship-to-Coast |
| 70 | 156.525 | 156.525 | *Digital Selective Distress, Safety, and Calling and Answering* |
| 71 | 156.575 | 156.575 | Non-commercial-Intership & Ship-to-Coast |
| 72 | 156.625 | 156.625 | Non-commercial-Intership (only) |
| 73 | 156.675 | 156.675 | Port Operations-Intership & Ship-to-Coast |
| 74 | 156.725 | 156.725 | Port Operations-Intership & Ship-to-Coast |
| 77 | 156.875 | 156.875 | Port Operations-Intership[8] |
| 78A | 156.925 | 156.925 | Non-commercial-Intership & Ship-to-Coast |
| 79A | 156.975 | 156.975 | Commercial- Intership & Ship-to-Coast[9] |
| 80A | 157.025 | 157.025 | Commercial- Intership & Ship-to-Coast[9] |
| 81A | 157.075 | 157.075 | *U.S. Government Use Only-* (USCG internal working channel) |
| 82A | 157.125 | 257.125 | *U.S. Government Use Only-* (USCG internal working channel) |
| 83A | 157.175 | 157.175 | *U.S. Government Use Only-* (USCG internal working channel) |
| 84 | 157.225 | 161.825 | Public Correspondence-(Marine Operator) |
| 85 | 157.275 | 161.875 | Public Correspondence-(Marine Operator) |
| 86 | 157.325 | 161.925 | Public Correspondence-(Marine Operator) |
| 87 | 157.375 | 161.975 | Public Correspondence-(Marine Operator) |
| 88 | 157.425 | 162.025 | Public Correspondence-(Marine Operator)[10] |
| 88A | 157.425 | 157.425 | Commercial- Intership[11] |

| Channel Number | Frequency (MHz) Transmit | Recieve | Communications Purpose |
|---|---|---|---|
| WX-1 | NA | 162.550 | Weather continuous broadcasts (Receive only) |
| WX-2 | NA | 162.400 | Weather continuous broadcasts (Receive only) |
| WX-3 | NA | 162.475 | Weather continuous broadcasts (Receive only) |
| WX-4 | NA | 162.425 | Weather continuous broadcasts[12] (Receive only) |
| WX-5 | NA | 162.450 | Weather continuous broadcasts[12] (Receive only) |
| WX-6 | NA | 162.500 | Weather continuous broadcasts[12] (Receive only) |
| WX-7 | NA | 162.525 | Weather continuous broadcasts[12] (Receive only) |

Notes:

1  Available for port operations and commercial communications only within Vessel Traffic Services (VTS) areas of New Orleans and Lower Mississippi River.

2  For VTS use in Seattle area.

3  For VTS use in designated port areas, and in the Great Lakes primarily for Ship Movement Service in the St. Lawrence Seaway; may be used in other areas on non-interference basis.

4  Primarily navigation safety between ships; available for VTS in Great Lakes; also used at drawbridges and canal locks.  Power limited to 1 watt; call signs omitted.  Not used in Lower Mississippi River.

5  Also used by Class C EPIRBs.

6  Used by state and local governments, power limited to 1 watt; may be used for Great Lakes weather broadcasts.

7  Navigational safety between ships in Lower Mississippi River.

8  Limited to communications with pilots regarding movement and docking of ships.  Power not to exceed 1 watt.

9  Also available for shared use by non-commercial vessels on the Great Lakes only.

10  In Puget Sound and Strait of Juan de Fuca and approaches only.

11  Only outside area of Puget Sound and Straight of Juan de Fuca and approaches.

12  Very seldom used.

# Appendix B
# Distress Message Procedure

1.   Make sure that your radio is turned on—turn squelch control back until you hear background noise.
2.   Make sure that you are tuned to VHF Channel 16 (or SSB 2182 kHz).
3.   Press microphone button, and speak slowly and clearly.
4.   Activate international radiotelephone alarm signal.
5.   Send your Distress Call:
     •   "mayday—mayday—mayday."
     •   "this is (name of your boat)—(name of your boat)—(name of your boat)—(call sign of the boat)."
     •   Make a brief pause—roughly three to five seconds.
     •   Send your Distress Message:
     •   "mayday—(name of your boat)."
     •   "my location is (latitude and longitude; or distance and direction from a known point)."
     •   describe the nature of your distress situation.
     •   describe the type of assistance you require.
     •   "my boat is (type, length, color of hull and trim, any other identifying features; state registration numbers)."
     •   "there are (number) persons on board—(number) adults [and (number) children, if any]."
     •   "there are no injuries" or "(state number of persons injured and briefly describe injuries or illness)."
     •   "I will listen on (Channel 16 or 2182 kHz as applicable)."
     •   "this is (name of the boat, call sign)."
     •   "over."
     Release the microphone button and wait for an answer.

WAIT FOR ABOUT 30 SECONDS FOR SOMEONE TO ANSWER; IF NO ANSWER IS HEARD, VERIFY THAT THE RADIO IS ON AND REPEAT THE DISTRESS CALL AND MESSAGE AS ABOVE.

IF NO ANSWER IS HEARD AFTER THREE CALLS, SWITCH TO ANOTHER CHANNEL AND MAKE THE CALL AGAIN THERE.

IMPORTANT!   In advance, fill in the name of the boat, the call sign, and its description—leave the other spaces blank at this time.  Make two copies; seal in plastic if possible.  Post one copy at or near the radio; put the other copy in a safe place that is known to other persons who are usually on board.

# INDEX

Numerals in *italics* indicate illustrations

## A

AC power, 10-11

Advanced Class License, 95, 96

Affirmative (procedure word), 53

Aircraft communications: EPIRB, 101-3, 105, *105*; SSB, 74; VHF channels (**06, 08, 09, 16, 18, 22A, 67, 68, 72, 88**), 24

Amateur (ham) radio, 7, 11, 79-80, 95-99; about, 97; channels and allocations, 97; equipment, 97-98, *98*; FCC regulations, 95; licenses, 95-96, 99; using, 99

Amplitude modulation (AM), 13, 71-72, 91

Antenna, 11, *11*, 13, *98*; amateur radio, 97-98, *98*; CB, 91, 94; cellular telephone, 109, 110, 111; EPIRB, 101; satellite, 114, 115, *115*, *116*

Antenna, SSB, 77, *78*, 80-84, *98*; installation, 81, *81*, 82, 83-84;maintenance, 84; and tuner, 80-81, *81*, 82, 83, 84, *98*

Antenna, VHF, *15*, 35, 54, *98*; fundamentals, 39-40, *40*, 41; gain, 40, *41*; installation, 41, 43-46, *42-45*; maintenance, 46, 47; for powerboats, 43-44; range, 40, *40*, 54; for sailboats, *43*, 45; for small boats, 39

Associated ship unit, 34

Audio power, 36

## B

Base-loaded whip antenna, *43*

Batteries, 11, *11*, 42, 43, 49, 67, *81*; cellular telephone,109; EPIRB, 103; hand-held transceiver, 39; internal nickel-cadmium, 11, 67; lead-acid storage, 10, 11

Bell System, 25

Break (procedure word), 53-54

Bridge-to-Bridge Channels (**13, 67**), 23-24, 37, 49, 5l, 62-63

Bridge-to-Bridge Communications, 61-62

Bridge-to-Bridge Radio Act, 20, 38

Broadcast Notice to Mariners, 8

## C

Calling Channel (**16**), 17, 19, 20, 21, 23, 36, 37, 38, 49, 50, 54, 56, 59, 60, 62, 63, 64, 65, 66, 73, 85, 94, 104

Call-sign identification, 50-52, 55, *55*, 56, 58, 86, 93

Canada, 29, 67, 78, 93, 115

Canal locks, 23

Caribbean, 78

CB Channel 9, 92, 94

Cellular telephones, 11, 107-12; about, 107-8, *108*; channels, 110; costs, 110, 111-12; equipment, *108*, 109-12; types of, for boats, 109, 110

Channels: amateur radio, 97; CB, 9l, 92-93, 94; cellular telephone, 110; EPIRB, 102, 104, 105, 106

Channels, SSB, 72-75; allocations, 73-75, 84-85, 86, 87, *87*; and choice of transceiver, 78-79; selection, 79-80

Channels, VHF, 14, 19-25; for aircraft use (**06, 08, 09, 16, 18, 22A, 67, 68, 72, 88**), 24; allocations, 14, 19-25; Bridge-to-Bridge Channels (**13, 67**), 23-24, 37, 62-63; Calling Channel (**16**), l7, 19, 20, 21, 23, 36, 37, 38, 49, 50, 54, 56, 59, 60, 62, 63, 64, 65, 66, 73, 85, 94, 104; call sign identification on, 50-52; Channel **70**, 25, 60; and choice of transceiver, 36-39; Coast Guard Working Channel (**22A**), 21, 61, 62;

**A**lfa
Diver Down;
Keep Clear

**K**ilo
Desire to Communicate

**B**ravo
Dangerous Cargo

**L**ima
Stop Instantly

**C**harlie
Yes

**M**ike
I Am Stopped

**D**elta
Keep Clear

**N**ovember
No

**E**cho
Altering Course to
Starboard

**O**scar
Man Overboard

**F**oxtrot
Disabled

**P**apa
About to Sail

**G**olf
Want a Pilot

**Q**uebec
Request Pratique

**H**otel
Pilot on Board

**R**omeo

**I**ndia
Altering Course to Port

**S**ierra
Engines Going Astern

**J**uliett
On Fire; Keep Clear

**T**ango
Keep Clear of Me